D1528548

THE GREAT
HISPANIC HERITAGE

Sammy Sosa

THE GREAT HISPANIC HERITAGE

Miguel de Cervantes

Cesar Chavez

Salvador Dali

Frida Kahlo

Pedro Martinez

Pablo Picasso

Juan Ponce de Leon

Diego Rivera

Carlos Santana

Sammy Sosa

Pancho Villa

THE GREAT
HISPANIC HERITAGE

Sammy Sosa

John Morrison

CHELSEA HOUSE
P U B L I S H E R S
An imprint of Infobase Publishing

Sammy Sosa

Chelsea House
An imprint of Infobase Publishing
132 West 31st Street
New York NY 10001

Library of Congress Cataloging-in-Publication Data

Morrison, John, 1929-
  Sammy Sosa / John Morrison.
      p. cm. — (Great Hispanic heritage)
  Includes bibliographical references and index.
  ISBN 0-7910-8845-6 (hard cover)
  1. Sosa, Sammy, 1968—Juvenile literature. 2. Baseball players—Dominican Republic—Biography—Juvenile literature. I. Title. II. Series.
  GV865.S59M67 2005
  796.357092—dc22   2005026236

Chelsea House books are available at special discounts when purchased in bulk quantities for businesses, associations, institutions, or sales promotions. Please call our Special Sales Department in New York at (212) 967-8800 or (800) 322-8755.

You can find Chelsea House on the World Wide Web at http://www.chelseahouse.com

Text design by Terry Mallon
Cover design by Keith Trego

Printed in the United States of America

Bang EJB 10 9 8 7 6 5 4 3 2 1

This book is printed on acid-free paper.

All links and web addresses were checked and verified to be correct at the time of publication. Because of the dynamic nature of the web, some addresses and links may have changed since publication and may no longer be valid.

Table of Contents

1   Shooting for a Record   6

2   Fortunate Son   16

3   Baseball Takes Center Stage   23

4   Sammy in Chicago   38

5   Coming into His Own   50

6   The History behind 61   59

7   The Race Is On   69

8   Sammy in the Community   79

9   Good-bye Chicago, Hello Baltimore   91

    Chronology and Timeline   101

    Notes   105

    Bibliography   107

    Further Reading/Web sites   108

    Index   109

Shooting
for a Record

The year 1998 was one of the most exciting in modern Major League Baseball history. When the season started that year, fans were wondering if a new home run record would be reached.

During the previous season, two players, Mark McGwire and Ken Griffey Jr., seemed on the verge of challenging Roger Maris's record of 61 homers, set 37 years before. But both ran out of time. McGwire, who split the 1997 season between the American League Oakland A's and the National League St. Louis Cardinals, had ended the season with 58 homers. Griffey, of the Seattle Mariners, had blasted 56.

What would 1998 bring? Would a new record be established, and which one of these great players would do it? Fans were in for a big surprise.

Major League Baseball was in dire need of a shot in the arm. The bitter baseball strike of 1994, which began on August 11 of that

Entering the 1998 season, Sammy Sosa was a dark-horse candidate to challenge Roger Maris's single-season home run record. However, on September 13, Sosa hit two home runs against the Milwaukee Brewers and joined St. Louis Cardinals first baseman Mark McGwire with 62 homers for the season, breaking Maris's 37-year-old record.

year and resulted in the cancellation of 920 games and the World Series, had left fans with a bitter taste in their mouths. Attendance plummeted. Not many people had sympathy for the striking ballplayers, who receive huge salaries—far beyond what the average fan could even dream of earning.

The issues were complicated, and not many fans even tried to understand them. All they knew was that the ballparks were closed and the annual excitement of pennant races, followed by the eagerly awaited World Series, was not part of their lives.

By 1997, the television ratings for the World Series had hit an all-time low. Only eight teams had matched the attendance figures they posted before the strike. It appeared that a lot of fans gave up on baseball entirely. The bitterness engendered by the strike was reminiscent of what happened in the wake of the 1919 "Black Sox" scandal. Eight players from the Chicago White Sox were banned from the sport for life after it was revealed that gamblers had paid them to throw the 1919 World Series. Back then, it took a man named George Herman "Babe" Ruth to restore fans' interest and confidence in the game. Ruth's spectacular career with the Boston Red Sox and the New York Yankees brought crowds back to the ballparks. His record of 60 home runs in a season, set in 1927, stood for 34 years, until broken in 1961 by Roger Maris, also a New York Yankee.

GAME STRATEGY

No one had gotten very close to Maris's record over those intervening years. One of the reasons is that hitting home runs never used to be a big part of baseball. Even in 1998, the average starter hit only about 17 home runs per season. Going further back, to Ruth's day, the average starter hit about six home runs. When Roger Maris and his Yankees teammate Mickey Mantle were blasting them out of the park, the average starter hit about 14 home runs. Until 1996, the only team to hit more than 225 home runs in a season was the Yankees in 1961. Yet since 1996, 26 teams have done it. What had changed to enable this to happen?

Baseball was—and still is—a game of strategy. In the past, batters were more interested in simply getting on base; advancing runners with base hits, sacrifice flies, or bunts; learning to hit behind a runner going to second base; or taking walks to get on base to be in a position to score. Hitting the ball over the fence was less of a priority. Managers favored and encouraged players who could do these relatively undramatic things, and had little patience with the ones who were more interested in their own records than helping the team.

Fans, on the other hand, love to see a baseball arc through the summer sky, climbing higher and higher only to come down amidst a shrieking crowd in the stands. They love to watch the batter trot coolly around the bases, taking in the cheers of the spectators. While the average fan might appreciate the strategies of the game, and even study them, give them a power hitter who can put the ball into the ozone, and most fans go wild.

That was the atmosphere in ballparks as the 1998 season began. Mark McGwire and Ken Griffey Jr. were the gladiators of the ballparks, and the people were eager to see them slay the ball.

SAMMY WHO?

In 1998, many fans never heard of, or at least knew very little about, a 29-year-old right fielder named Sammy Sosa. But they soon would. As the 1998 season began, Sosa had already been in the major leagues for 10 years. He was playing for the Chicago Cubs, a team that its own fans thought of mostly as a "lovable loser"; a team that had not won a World Series since 1908.

Sosa was a veteran with an uneven record. He had enormous talent and was personable, always smiling and anxious to please. But he had problems on the field that made people, especially managers and teammates, wonder if he would ever be the superstar he seemed to have the potential to be. Sosa was a wild swinger who struck out too often. He didn't seem to want to be walked, even if a walk might advance a runner. He seemed to scorn base hits, preferring always to swing for the fences. And he seemed more willing to strike out than take a walk. As an outfielder, he had a tremendous arm. He could throw the ball very far, but he often threw over the head of the cutoff man or to the wrong base. Throughout much of his early career, he didn't seem to understand how to become a well-rounded player, a trait that would ultimately serve to help his team win more games.

But Sosa began to mature as a player with the Chicago Cubs, the team he joined in 1992 after mediocre performances with two other teams. The Cubs were willing to work with him and to try to make him into a more complete ballplayer, while encouraging him and making him feel welcome. Gradually, over the years, the lessons began to take hold. His batting average improved, and he seemed more willing to do things to help the team, even if it meant sacrificing some personal numbers.

In 1993, he became only the tenth player in National League history to accomplish a "30/30"—hitting more than 30 home runs and stealing more than 30 bases in one season. He did it again in 1995. When the 1997 season began, Sosa's hitting coach, Billy Williams, said, "I have confidence that Sammy will improve. He's already become a much more patient and intelligent hitter."[1] And his own confidence in his abilities was evident when a reporter asked him if he thought he could hit 50 home runs in 1997. "Why not 60?"[2] he replied.

However, Sammy's 1997 season gave little indication that he could challenge anyone for a home run record. He hit 39 home runs, not 60. His batting average was .251. He got 161 hits, including 31 doubles and four triples. But he also struck out 174 times in 642 at-bats, indicating that he had not gotten over his habit of swinging at bad pitches. While Sammy's 1997 numbers were nothing to be ashamed of, his statistics were not on par with those of the league's superstars. However, he went into the 1998 season with a new contract—$42.5 million over four years—that might have served as motivation. And he had a new hitting coach, Jeff Pentland, who began to show Sammy some ways to improve his hitting.

LATINO IDOL

Everything would change the following year—the fateful year of 1998—when Sammy would prove that he was indeed a superstar. He would become one of those heroes expected to perform incredible deeds. He would become the idol of the Latino communities in the United States and, especially, in Latin America—particularly his home country of the Dominican Republic, a small nation that has sent a remarkable number of baseball players to the United States and the major leagues.

Sammy Sosa came swooping out of the Midwest in 1998 to surprise everyone with his power as he gradually gained on the home run leaders, eventually leaving Ken Griffey Jr. in his dust and bearing down on Mark McGwire. When that amazing season ended, both Sosa and McGwire had far exceeded Roger Maris's record of 61 home runs—McGwire with an incredible 70 and Sosa with 66. Griffey had faded out of the race and finished with 56, the same number he had hit in 1997. Despite losing the home run contest to McGwire, Sosa was voted the National League's 1998 Most Valuable Player by the Baseball Writers Association. The very next year, he hit 63 home runs, but once again was bested by "Big Mac" McGwire, who hit 65. (The Giants' Barry Bonds went on to break McGwire's record with 73 home runs in 2001.)

There was no question that Sammy Sosa, the kid who grew up poor in the poverty-stricken city of San Pedro de Macoris, in the equally impoverished Dominican Republic, had reached the level of superstar. He would remain at that level for many years, going on to become the only player in major league history to hit more than 60 home runs in three seasons—1998, 1999, and 2001.

THE MILLIONAIRE

By the time he was traded to the Baltimore Orioles before the 2005 season, Sosa had 574 career home runs and needed only 26 more to reach 600. He had nine straight seasons in which he

Sammy Sosa waves a Dominican flag during a parade held in his honor in New York on October 17, 1998. Sosa, a native of San Pedro de Macoris, was presented with a key to New York by Mayor Rudolph Giuliani and October 17 was declared "Sammy Sosa Day" in the city with the largest Dominican community outside the Dominican Republic.

had 100 or more RBI (runs batted in, also called "ribbies"). In June 1998, he hit 20 home runs, besting the all-time record of 18 home runs in one month set by the Detroit Tigers' Rudy York in 1937. The boy who had to shine shoes and wash cars in the streets of his hometown to help support his family also became a multimillionaire. He became a philanthropist who gives generously to help others—both in the United States and in his native land—through such endeavors as his Sammy Sosa Charitable Foundation.

After the 1998 season, Sosa was given a ticker-tape parade in New York City, he helped President Bill Clinton light a Christmas tree in Washington, D.C., and he received a standing ovation from Congress when Clinton introduced him during a

State of the Union address. He was honored by Pope John Paul II during the pope's visit to New York for the work of his foundation in organizing relief efforts in the Dominican Republic after it was devastated by Hurricane Georges in 1998. President George W. Bush once said that when he was a managing general partner of the Texas Rangers, Sosa's first team in the major leagues, "My biggest mistake was trading Sammy Sosa."[3] When the prime minister of Japan, Keizo Obuchi, arrived in Chicago in 1998, he said the first person he wanted to meet was Sammy Sosa.

BLOWING KISSES

Of equal importance to Sammy, however, was the way he was honored by the people of San Pedro de Macoris, where entire neighborhoods would gather to listen to his games on small radios and pour into the streets in celebration after his every accomplishment. They called him the *Bambino el del Caribe*— "the Bambino (Babe Ruth's nickname) of the Caribbean."

For a long time, Sosa charmed fans in the Cubs' legendary Wrigley Field by his quirky little gestures after he hit the ball. As he explained to the *National Magazine of the Successful American Latino* in December 2003: "I touch my heart with a two-finger salute after getting a hit and then I blow kisses, one for my mother and one more for the family and relatives back home." His uniform number was 21, the number worn by his hero, the great Pittsburgh slugger and humanitarian Roberto Clemente, a native of Puerto Rico.

Sosa also expected to be treated like the superstar he was. He had his personal valet in uniform to wait on him, and the boom box he played at ear-splitting decibels in the Wrigley Field clubhouse, belting out salsa music along with Michael Jackson and Britney Spears songs, was only tolerated by his teammates.

That fans and fellow players began to find these quirks and gestures less charming and, eventually, annoying, as Sosa's production at the plate faltered in later years, is part of the tragedy of Sammy's final seasons in Chicago. Though it is very likely that Sosa will be voted into the National Baseball Hall of Fame someday, his final years with the Chicago Cubs were a disappointment to him and his fans. Sosa's slow slide into disfavor probably began when he broke a bat during a game with Tampa Bay on June 3, 2003. The bat was lined with cork, which makes the bat lighter and enables the user to hit the ball farther. Using a corked bat is against baseball's rules, and the league suspended Sosa for seven games. When Sammy came to the plate after he returned to Chicago, he was booed by fans. There were cries of "Cheater!" Some fans threw corks at him.

Sosa insisted he had picked up the corked bat by mistake. He said it was a bat he used for batting practice and he didn't mean to use it in a game. X-ray tests of 76 other bats in Sosa's possession found no cork, and five of his record-setting bats in the National Baseball Hall of Fame also showed no cork. But Sammy was upset by the reaction of fans. He wasn't used to getting booed, particularly not in his home ballpark of Wrigley Field. He had thought of the fans as part of his family. He loved them and he thought they loved him.

"I want to make it clear that hopefully they forget," Sosa told reporters in Philadelphia after the corked-bat incident. "I have to deal with that for the rest of my life, no question. But I'm only human. I'm not the only guy in this world that made a mistake. Hopefully, they'll forget and just let me continue to make people happy."[4]

Then in 2005, there were the accusations of steroid use. Although there has never been any evidence that Sammy Sosa used performance-enhancing drugs, he and Mark McGwire were among those called to testify about steroid use in Major League Baseball before a congressional committee. Naturally, many fans thought the worst, and Sammy was put in the uncomfortable position of being asked repeatedly about performance-enhancing drugs, substances that he has vigorously denied ever using.

Sammy Sosa's career, including its highs and lows, has been

in many ways emblematic of the story of baseball itself over recent years. Throughout his years in the major leagues, he has brought excitement to the game, and his infectious smile and positive attitude have won him fans worldwide. The story of Sammy's success is a story of one man's journey from humble beginnings to the height of fame and fortune, and one that is a tribute to his talent, drive, and winning personality.

Fortunate Son

It would be hard to imagine a greater contrast than that among the great home run hitters who set out in 1998 to challenge long-established and venerable hitting records. Mark McGwire, son of a well-off dentist in California, started playing Little League ball at an early age and learned the game from a series of experienced coaches. Ken Griffey Jr., son of a star outfielder with the great Cincinnati Reds teams of the mid-1970s, practically cut his teeth on baseball. As a child, he hung out with the sons of other players and got to know some of the stars of that era, such as Johnny Bench, Pete Rose, Tony Perez, Joe Morgan, Dave Concepción, and George Foster. And there was Sammy Sosa, who grew up poor in the Dominican Republic and didn't begin playing baseball until he was 14. When Griffey and McGwire were honing their skills on local baseball diamonds, Sammy Sosa was just beginning to learn the fundamentals on the rock-strewn playgrounds of San Pedro

A Dominican boy hits a tennis ball with a broken bat during an informal baseball game in San Pedro de Macoris. Like most Dominican boys, Sammy played baseball as a child, but most of his time was spent helping support his family by shining shoes and sweeping the floors of a local factory.

de Macoris with a glove given to him by a shoeshine customer. "My life is kind of like a miracle,"[5] Sosa once said.

Samuel Peralta Sosa was born on November 12, 1968, in the town of Consuelo in the Dominican Republic, a beautiful country with an ancient and troubled history. He was the fifth of the six children born to Juan Bautista Montero and Lucretia Sosa, called Mireya.

Consuelo is a small farming town approximately 50 miles east of Santo Domingo, the capital. Sammy's father, Juan Bautista Montero, drove a tractor in the sugarcane fields around Consuelo. His mother, Mireya, had a son, Luis, by a

(*continued on page 20*)

A PROUD TRADITION OF BASEBALL IN LATIN AMERICA

Although Sammy Sosa had visions of becoming the next great heavy-weight boxer, many Latin American children dream of playing in the major leagues. Baseball has been a part of the Latin American stream of conscience since shortly after the first organized leagues were established in the United States in the 1840s. According to a story in the *San Francisco Examiner*, the first baseball game in Latin America was probably played in Cuba. In 1866, sailors on an American ship taking on sugar in Havana invited Cuban longshoremen to join them in a game of baseball. In two years, the Cubans became so fond of the sport that they formed a league. One of the teams was Club Habana (Havana), and one of its founders, Esteban Bellan, became the first Latino to play in the United States. A catcher, he played three seasons (1871–1873) with the Tory Haymakers and New York Mutuals in the National Association, which later became the National League.

The history of baseball in Latin America is of particular interest today because about 25 percent of Major League Baseball players are Latino. The Dominican Republic, birthplace of Sammy Sosa, sends more players to the major leagues than all other Latin American countries combined. In 1902, Colombian-born Luis Castro became a second base-man for the Philadelphia Athletics. In 1923, Adolfo Luque, called the "Pride of Havana," became the first Latino pitcher to win more than 20 games in the major leagues. He won 27 for the Cincinnati Reds. However, it wasn't until Jackie Robinson broke the color barrier in the United States with the Brooklyn Dodgers in 1947 that black and dark-skinned Latinos could think about playing Major League Baseball in the United States.

Ozzie Virgil, who played catcher, third base, and the outfield for the New York Giants, starting in 1956, was the first Dominican to play in the big leagues. In 1983, New York Giants pitcher Juan Marichal, who was born in the Dominican Republic, became the first living Latin American ballplayer inducted into the Hall of Fame. (Cuban-born Martin Dihigo, who played for several teams in the Negro Leagues in the 1920s, 1930s, and 1940s, was inducted posthumously in 1977. He died in 1971.)

The domination of Latin players in the major leagues surged between 1960 and 1970. Here are some of the highlights of that period:

Zoilo Versalles won the American League Most Valuable Player award in 1965; Roberto Clemente won the National League MVP in 1966, as well as three batting titles; Luis Aparicio won nine straight base-stealing crowns; Vic Power won Gold Gloves from 1960 to 1964; Tony Oliva won the 1964 Rookie of the Year award; Orlando Cepeda won both the Comeback Player of the Year in 1966 and National League MVP in 1967; and pitcher Juan Marichal led the National League in wins with 25 in 1963 and 26 in 1968.

And one of the remarkable facts about the Latin players, then and now, is that most of them grew up poor and had to struggle through their early lives just to eat and have a roof over their heads. They learned the game on rock-strewn playgrounds with makeshift equipment. The American major league teams freely exploited many of the young Latin players. They received paltry signing bonuses, compared to the American rookies, and 90 to 95 percent of those who arrived in the United States for tryouts with major league teams never made it.

Marcos Breton, the highly regarded Latino sportswriter for the *Sacramento Bee*, who helped Sammy Sosa write his autobiography, cited one team official as admitting the Latino players were taken advantage of. Writing in an article in *ColorLines* in spring 2000, Breton quoted Dick Balderson, vice president of the Colorado Rockies, as calling this practice the "boatload mentality." "Instead of signing four American guys at $25,000 each, you sign 20 Dominican guys for $5,000 each," Balderson was quoted as saying.

Sammy Sosa's signing bonus for a contract with the Texas Rangers in 1985 was $3,500. Coincidentally, that was the same amount that Jackie Robinson got to sign with the Dodgers in 1946, almost 40 years earlier.

(*continued from page 17*)

previous marriage that ended in divorce. Sammy never referred to Luis as anything but his older brother. It was Luis who eventually talked him into playing baseball. On August 30, 1975, when Sammy was six, his father died, leaving Mireya, Sammy, and his six siblings to survive on their own. Sammy and his siblings took their mother's maiden name, a custom in some parts of the country.

Sammy's father had been a big fan of the local baseball team, Licey—one of the better teams in the Dominican Winter League. But there wasn't much time for the Sosa children even to watch baseball, let alone play it, because of the struggle just to keep food on the table and a roof over their heads. Every member of the family who was old enough had to pitch in to make money. Luis was 14, and much of the burden of supporting the family fell on him and his mother. Mireya cooked for other people, sold lottery tickets, and cleaned houses to support her family.

SHOE-SHINE BOYS

Luis was Sammy's hero. He followed his older brother around and helped out when he could. They would go to the business section of town and shine shoes. They also would head to the nicer neighborhoods, find a nice car, and wash it. That meant waiting, sometimes for hours, for the owner to return to his car and, with luck, pay them. Not all of them paid, and all those hours were wasted.

Despite the hard work, the family often went hungry. Sammy recalled in his autobiography that sometimes they had only two meals a day, and ate a lot of rice and beans, fried plantains, and yucca. This kind of diet was not good for a future athlete, and one of the obstacles Sammy had to overcome was that malnourishment had weakened him. When he was hitting balls many years later for a major league scout, his hits would die in the outfield. The scout was familiar with the problem that malnourishment causes.

In 1978, the family moved to Santo Domingo, the capital.

Because they were poor, they were forced to live in a neighborhood with other poor people. They slept in one room in a shack with dirt floors. In fact, it would be a long time before Sammy lived with anything but dirt floors in his home.

The big city was a scary place compared to Consuelo. Drugs were plentiful, and many of the teenagers were in gangs. There was garbage and sewage in the streets, and too much crime. However, Mireya was able to make money preparing food and washing clothes for the more prosperous residents. After nine months, however, Mireya decided to move out of the dangerous city to a quieter place. In 1981, they moved to San Pedro de Macoris. Sammy was 12 and it was time for him to go to work to help the family.

He and his brothers staked out a place in the town's main square and started shining the shoes of business executives who worked in the sugar industry or in the factories of Zona Franca, an industrial park. There was a lot of competition and the kids would fight among themselves for customers. The Sosa brothers believed they did the best job shining shoes, and they developed a loyal clientele. One of their customers was a man named William Chase, an American from Bristol, Maine, who owned a shoe factory. Chase was so impressed by the hardworking Sosa boys that he offered them jobs in his factory.

They were put to work sweeping the factory floors. Working 8 A.M. to 4 P.M., Sammy could bring home 300 pesos a week, a lot of money for a poor kid at that time. Sammy's schooling had for years been random at best, and now, since he had a full-time job, he dropped out of school in the eighth grade and never went back.

FIRST DREAMS

Chase and his wife became like surrogate parents to the Sosa boys. They would give them presents and, after a meal in a local restaurant, would give them leftover food to take home to their family. When Sammy was 12, Chase gave the boy he knew as Mikey his first bicycle. Of course, Chase expected the boys to work for him in return for his money and gifts, and they did.

As he recounted in his autobiography, Sammy told of a Mother's Day when he wanted desperately to give his mother something special. But he had no money. For the first time, he went out into the streets and started begging. He made enough money to buy his mother a cigarette—one cigarette. He recalls saying to her, "Mommy, I don't have much to give you, but I give you this with all my heart on Mother's Day."

She was thrilled. "What a beautiful present," she replied.

"I've given her so much since then," Sammy wrote, "but that might have been the most meaningful thing I ever did for her—it came straight from my heart."

One day when Sammy was about 13, Chase gave him a baseball mitt that he had purchased during a trip to the United States. It was blue and cost about $100, a lot of money at that time.

Even though he was grateful for the present, Sammy wasn't really interested in baseball. His dream was to be a boxer. His great heroes were Sugar Ray Leonard, Thomas Hearns, and Marvin Hagler. He started attending a boxing school in the city. He would get up early and do roadwork, then spar and pummel the speed bag and heavy bag at the school.

"I thought I had what it took to be a fighter," he said in his autobiography, "but, fortunately for me, the people who loved me the most had other ideas."

Paramount among those was his mother, who quickly scotched the idea. After a serious sit-down talk with her, Sammy abandoned the idea of a boxing career.

3

Baseball Takes Center Stage

When his boxing dreams ended, Sammy turned to baseball, and the rest, as they say, is history. He threw himself into baseball the way he threw himself into everything he did. Sammy got permission from Bill Chase to play a couple of days a week on work time. Eventually, he was spending all his time practicing baseball. The ever-generous Chase hired Sammy's younger brothers, so the family wouldn't lose any income.

One of the factors that motivated Sammy at that point was seeing some of the big league players from San Pedro around town. "I would see major league players from the Dominican, such as Joaquin Andujar, Julio Franco, and George Bell," he said. "They would build beautiful houses. People would come up to them. They were always in the middle of a crowd. And I can remember thinking it would be nice to live like that."[6]

A PASSION FOR BASEBALL

Baseball is a passion in the Dominican Republic, probably more so than in any other Latin country. It is played year-round, with amateur leagues taking the field in the summer and professional teams in the winter. And for some mysterious reason, San Pedro de Macoris, where the Sosa family eventually settled, has sent more than its share of great players to the major leagues in the United States.

San Pedro de Macoris is a crowded city of about 125,000 residents on the Caribbean Sea. One of the town's claims to fame is the Malecon, a wide, seaside boardwalk along the beautiful clear-blue Caribbean that is a promenade for visitors and the more prosperous locals. The other is baseball. Vacationing tourists can visit the fields where many of the major league stars who once lived in San Pedro de Macoris learned the fundamentals of the game. There are also games to watch, with some pretty high-caliber talent on display. In the summer, there are amateur league games, and in the winter, the primary season, many major leaguers arrive from the United States to compete with local stars in the Dominican Winter League. There are numerous training fields operated by major league teams looking for Dominican talent, and Japanese teams also have a facility.

In addition to Bell and Sosa, other major league stars who were born or grew up in San Pedro de Macoris include short-stops Julio Franco and Tony Fernandez; outfielder Rico Carty; third baseman Pedro Guerrero; and second baseman Juan Samuel.

AN INTERESTING HISTORY

The Dominican Republic occupies the eastern two-thirds of the island of Hispaniola, in the West Indies. Haiti takes up the island's western end. Hispaniola traces its history back to Christopher Columbus. The great Genoese explorer landed on the island in December 1492, on his first voyage to the New World. He had been looking for a sea route to Asia and didn't know he had discovered a new world. When he realized that

Cuba was not Japan, he pushed on to the island that he named Hispaniola. Some historians believe that Columbus is buried in the Cathedral of Santo Domingo.

Agriculture, especially sugarcane, and tourism are the Dominican Republic's chief sources of income. Refineries produce approximately one million tons of sugar a year, most of which is shipped to the United States. The fluctuating price of sugar has led frequently to economic problems and the closing of many refineries. The country is largely poor—more than half of the people live at or below the poverty level. During much of its history, the Dominican Republic was ruled by either harsh dictators or other countries. U.S. troops occupied the country twice in the 1900s to put down violence among political groups, and U.S. Marines occupied the country from 1916 to 1934.

In 1930, Rafael Leonidas Trujillo Molina seized power in a military revolt and ruled the Dominican Republic ruthlessly for 30 years. He allowed little freedom, and killed and tortured many people who opposed him. Trujillo was, however, a great baseball fan. In 1936, when he had been in power for seven years, his son, Ramfis, took control of Licey, one of the two professional baseball teams in Santo Domingo. He was upset when his team was defeated in the national championships that year by the team from San Pedro de Macoris. His father was even more upset. He hated San Pedro because it was a hotbed of opposition to his regime. So the following year Ramfis combined Licey with Escogido, the other team from Santo Domingo, into what was supposed to be a super team. It was called the Ciudad Trujillo Dragones, and it was designed to restore the Trujillo family honor.

But scouts from San Pedro had a different plan. They flew to Pittsburgh to sign the top players of the Pittsburgh Crawfords, part of the famed Negro League. Among those signed were such legendary black players as pitcher Satchel Paige, Josh Gibson, and Cool Papa Bell. When the players and scouts arrived in the Dominican Republic, they were met by

Rafael Leonidas Trujillo Molina seized power of the Dominican Republic in 1930 and ruled as president until he was assassinated in 1961. Molina was a big baseball fan and once forced Negro League players from the United States to play for his son's team, the Ciudad Trujillo Dragones.

Trujillo's troops. The scouts were thrown in jail and the black players were informed that they would be playing for Ciudad Trujillo.

Paige, Gibson, and Bell were joined on Ciudad Trujillo by several other top Negro League players, including Perucho Cepeda, father of future Hall of Famer Orlando Cepeda. At the same time, another team, Domingo, entered the picture and signed up some of the greatest Latino stars of the day, not only from the Dominican Republic but also Venezuela, Mexico, Cuba, and elsewhere.

THE NEGRO LEAGUES

The Negro Leagues were a collection of professional baseball leagues made up of predominantly black teams. The reason for their existence was segregation—before 1947, organized base-ball had an unwritten policy that excluded African-American baseball players from its teams. The Pittsburgh Crawfords of the Negro National League became one of the most powerful and popular teams in black baseball when it was taken over in 1935 by Gus Greenlee, a gambler and numbers racketeer. Greenlee built a team that attracted large numbers of fans by hiring some of the finest talent of the Negro Leagues. They included the three men—Satchel Paige, Josh Gibson, and Cool Papa Bell—who traveled to the Dominican Republic in 1937 to play for a team controlled by the dictator Rafael Trujillo.

Satchel Paige was one of the most talented and colorful players ever to play baseball. He had pet names for his pitches, like the "Bat Dodger," "Hesitation Pitch," and "Nothing Pitch." He started playing in the Negro Leagues in 1927, and, in his 40s, got a chance to play in the major leagues, with the Cleveland Indians, St. Louis Browns, and Kansas City Athletics. Cool Papa Bell said of Paige, "He made his living by throwing the ball to a spot over the plate the size of a matchbook cover."

Bell, whose real name was James Thomas Bell, played in the Negro Leagues for 20 years. He was known for his speed on the bases and as a great leadoff batter, which meant he knew how to get on base.

Josh Gibson was a power hitter, famous for his mammoth home runs. His career batting average of .426 is an all-time record. He died just three months before Jackie Robinson started the integration of Major League Baseball with the Brooklyn Dodgers. All of these men are members of the National Baseball Hall of Fame.

The hard-fought games played in 1937 among Ciudad Trujillo, San Pedro de Macoris, and Domingo are legendary and still remembered to this day. After Ciudad Trujillo lost the opening game to San Pedro, Satchel Paige recalled that his team was surrounded by troops, firing their guns in the air, and shouting, "The Benefactor (Trujillo) doesn't like to lose!" The Americans were put in jails the night before each game to insure that they were well rested.

Ciudad Trujillo managed to knock off Santiago during the regular season and faced San Pedro in a seven-game series for the championship. Taken from their prison cells to Quisqueya Stadium each day, the American players were so nervous that they dropped the first three games. Paige was firmly convinced that if the Dragones lost the series, they would all face firing squads. He was so upset, he had to gobble antacid pills during the entire series.

Fortunately, the Dragones escaped the firing squad by winning the next four games to take the championship. A jubilant festival ensued. But the country had financial problems after buying some of the top players, and professional baseball in the Dominican Republic came to an end for 14 years. Professional baseball returned to the island in 1951 and has been played ever since. Today, many players in the major leagues come from towns in the Dominican Republic, including Sammy Sosa.

SAMMY GETS HIS START

Sammy was 14 when he started playing for an amateur team run by a man named Hector Peguero. He had been introduced to Hector by his brother Luis, who was playing on the team. Hector knew that Sammy had a strong arm and could hit a baseball, but he declared him a "lobo," meaning wild and raw. Peguero, who became a lifelong friend of Sammy's, tried to take some of the wildness out of him. During a game in a park named after Rico Carty, the great Atlanta Braves outfielder and a San Pedro native, Sammy hit his first home run. Then he hit another, a grand slam. "In every game he would do something to surprise me," Peguero said. "And he would always hit the ball hard."[7]

Because of all the great players who come from the Dominican Republic, many major league teams visit the island to recruit players. More than 20 major league teams now have baseball-training camps, and scouts from these teams are sent out to hold tryouts throughout the island. Those who are lucky enough to be offered a contract are usually young men between the ages of 17 and 18. If a recruit shows promise, he is promoted to the minor league system in the United States, with the hope of making it to the major leagues. Nothing is guaranteed, and out of the hundreds who are recruited, only a small proportion make it.

In 1984, when Sammy was 15, a Philadelphia Phillies scout named Francisco Acevedo offered Sammy a contract. He signed it for a $2,500 bonus. But nothing ever came of it, and Sammy never got his money. He learned later that the contract had not been sent to the United States. No reason was ever given, but Sammy's initial hopes for a career in the major leagues had been cruelly dashed.

THE TEXAS RANGERS COME CALLING

Shortly thereafter, Sammy was offered a tryout with the New York Yankees in nearby San Cristobal. These tryouts consisted of running the 60-yard dash, taking batting practice, running in the outfield, shagging fly balls, and demonstrating arm strength. The situation with the Yankees seemed promising. The scouts were impressed by Sammy's skills, but suddenly he was ordered to take off his uniform and leave. The scouts never told him why he had to leave. There were more frustrations ahead. A scout for the Atlanta Braves took a look at his skinny physique one day and said, "I don't sign undersized players."[8] He practiced at training camps run by scouts for the Montreal Expos, the New York Mets, and the Toronto Blue Jays, all without success.

Unknown to Sammy, however, two scouts from the Texas Rangers—Amado Dinzey and Omar Minaya—were tracking his progress. Minaya, who would later become general manager of the New York Mets, was coaching in the Gulf Coast League in Florida when Dinzey told him about Sammy, whom he had seen a couple of years before. Minaya flew to Puerto Plata, where the Rangers had a training facility, and invited Sammy to come for a tryout.

Puerto Plata is a three-hour bus ride from San Pedro. After he arrived and started to work out there, Minaya saw that Sammy was a free-swinger and he liked his spirit. But he noticed that Sammy's hits died in the outfield. He knew what that meant from seeing other young Dominican players—he was undernourished. Minaya was also not impressed by Sammy's speed. He was clocked at 7.5 seconds in the 60-yard dash. Scouts were looking for players who could run the 60 in less than 5.8 seconds. However, despite his doubts, and after talking it over with Amado Dinzey, who agreed that Sammy had tremendous potential, they decided to offer him a contract with the Rangers. This time it was the real thing. "I was a professional," Sammy wrote in his autobiography. "I had finally made it."

When the Rangers' check for $3,500 arrived, Sammy told his mother, "Mom, we're millionaires!"

Bill Chase gave Sammy a set of dumbbells and barbells so he could start adding muscle to his skinny frame. Sammy began using them every day. He also began running on the beach to improve his speed. In February 1986, the Rangers held a practice in Santo Domingo to evaluate their prospects and decide who would go to spring training in the United States the following March. Sammy was among those picked and he took his first plane ride from Santo Domingo International Airport. He landed in Miami and took a flight to Plant City, Florida, where the Rangers trained.

He was in the United States, and he was on his way to a Major League Baseball career. It was a dream come true for the skinny kid who just a short time before was shining shoes, sweeping up in a shoe factory, and living in a house with dirt floors. He was paid $700 a month during spring training, and he sent most of it back home to his family.

Sammy could speak little English, and he felt like a shrimp. He wrote, "I would look around and think, 'Damn, these American players are big.'" But he felt he was hitting the ball well and learning the fundamentals of the Rangers' system. When spring training ended, he rushed to the bulletin board where the names of those who were to stay with the organization were posted. He was relieved when he saw his name at the very bottom of the second page in tiny print: "Sosa." He had made it! Sammy didn't know it at the time, but the odds were against him. Some 90 to 95 percent of foreign-born baseball prospects are released at the Class-A level.

Sosa was sent to Daytona Beach, Florida, for extended spring training, and then reported to his new Rookie League team, Sarasota. He played 61 games in Sarasota, hit 4 home runs, had a .275 batting average, and stole 11 bases. His speed on the bases had improved and became one of his greatest assets. In 1987, the Rangers sent him to a Class-A team in Gastonia, North Carolina. He did so well that he and his friend Juan Gonzalez, who would later win the American League's Most Valuable Player award in 1996 and 1998, were picked to play in the South Atlantic League All-Star game in Knoxville, Tennessee.

Sammy had a .279 batting average in Gastonia, hit 11 home runs, and collected 59 RBI. The next year, the Rangers sent him to the Florida State League, the highest level of Class-A ball. He was 19. Although his batting average was an anemic .229, he stole 42 bases and led the league in triples. He struck out 106 times because he was still a free-swinger and chased a lot of bad pitches—a habit that would dog him for most of his career. He would swing at pitches in the dirt or over his head. A coach once told him his strike zone appeared to be from the top of his head to his feet. *(continued on page 34)*

A CIRCLE OF FRIENDS

LATINO PLAYERS HELP EACH OTHER ACHIEVE SUCCESS IN THE MAJOR LEAGUES

Back when they were all hungry Latino kids yearning to make it in the American major leagues, Sammy Sosa, Juan Gonzalez, Rey Sanchez, and Felipe Castillo were also just plain hungry. In his autobiography, Sammy tells about the time in 1986 when they were all vying for jobs with the Texas Rangers and playing in the Rookie League in Sarasota, Florida. They practiced in Daytona and discovered a Chinese restaurant there that offered all-you-can-eat food. "During extended spring training, Sunday was our only day off," Sammy wrote, "so we would all go there. . . . I remember the owner couldn't believe how much we could eat. And after a while, he'd see us coming and yell, 'No, no! No ballplayers! You eat too much!'"*

Sammy had many Latino friends during his career, and they learned the game and how to conduct themselves in the United States and the big leagues from each other. In Florida, Sammy and Puerto Rican-born Juan Gonzalez, who would go on to have great years as a slugging outfielder for the Texas Rangers and other teams, were especially close.

Omar Minaya, the scout who discovered Sammy, recalled in Sosa's autobiography, "The amazing thing about these two guys was that the first time they met, they kind of gravitated to each other, and pretty soon they were in the outfield playing catch. The first time they played catch professionally, they played with each other—Sammy Sosa and Juan Gonzalez. But you have to remember that at that point, they still faced a long road to the major leagues. Yet you could tell the talent was there." "Juan was a sixteen-year-old kid from Puerto Rico," Minaya added, "and was kind of in the same boat as Sammy. He was maybe a little more advanced because up to that point, he had played in more organized baseball than Sammy."**

Infielder Rey Sanchez, also Puerto Rican-born, would go on to a successful career with the Chicago Cubs and other teams, playing in 2004 with the Tampa Devil Rays and in 2005 with the New York Yankees.

Another pal in those days was Mickey Cruz, who, unfortunately, didn't make it to the majors. The rookies, all teenagers, roomed together in rather small quarters. "We all lived together and did everything together," Sammy wrote in his autobiography.

Sammy was linked later in his career with the great pitcher Pedro Martinez, even though they played in different leagues, Sammy with the Chicago Cubs in the National League and Martinez mostly with the Boston Red Sox in the American League. But both grew up poor in the Dominican Republic, Sammy in San Pedro de Macoris and Martinez in the town of Manoguayabo, 50 miles away, and they could share stories about learning the game on the dusty playgrounds of their youth. "Dominican Dominators," said a headline in *Latino Legends In Sports* in 2001, which described the two superstars. Ozzie Gonzalez wrote in that issue:

> These men are not huge in stature, but sheer power runs through their bodies when it's time to attack their opponent in close games. Fans look on in total amazement at how these two Dominican Dominators, Sammy Sosa and Pedro Martinez, continue to buzz saw the competition and become the baseball darlings of Latin America and modern day heroes to America.***

When Sammy got to the Texas Rangers in 1989, Ruben Sierra was playing Sammy's favorite position in right field. The Puerto Rican-born Sierra, who was three years older than Sammy, had a great season that year, batting .306 and hitting 29 home runs. It would have been hard to dislodge him, but fellow Dominican Julio Franco, the hard-hitting short-stop, got wind of Sammy's ambition. "He would look over at Ruben and whisper to me, 'Tell him. Tell him,'" Sammy wrote in his autobiography. "Julio was really egging me on. So I did it. I said, 'Ruben, you better start getting used to center field because right field is mine.'"†

Sammy didn't stay with Texas long enough to dislodge Sierra, but this story was typical of the kind of lighthearted interplay that went on between the Latino players with whom Sammy was associated in his early years and who were helping him learn the intricacies of the game, master a new language, and fit in with the American way of life.

---

* Sammy Sosa, *Sosa: An Autobiography* (New York: Warner Books, 2000), 79.
** Ibid., 75.
*** http://www.latinosportslegends.com/sosa-martinez_dominators.htm
† Sosa, 93.

(*continued from page 31*)

Going First-class

Sammy went back home and played in the Dominican Winter League that year with Escogido, one of the best teams in the league. He hit .279 and was second in the league in RBI. He was named the league's Rookie of the Year. His team won the league championship and went to Mazatlan, Mexico, for the Caribbean World Series.

At the end of the season, the Rangers invited him to their major league spring training. For the first time, he got to fly first-class and stay in a fancy hotel. He was getting his first taste of life in the big leagues. After spring training in Florida, Sammy was sent to play with the Tulsa Drillers, the Rangers' AA Texas League team in Tulsa, Oklahoma. After 66 games with the Drillers, he was batting .297 with seven home runs and 31 RBI. At this point, he got the break he was waiting for. Pete Incaviglia, the Rangers' power-hitting outfielder, hurt his neck and the team needed a replacement. They looked around their minor league system and chose Sammy Sosa.

Sammy's first major league game was a doubleheader to be played in legendary Yankee Stadium, the "house that Ruth built." It was June 16, 1989, a muggy, overcast day at the stadium. Sosa would lead off against Yankee pitcher Andy Hawkins. He was the first pitcher Sammy faced in the major leagues, and he hit a single. In the sixth inning, he hit a double against Hawkins. He had a good day, but the Rangers lost, 10-3. They also lost the nightcap, 6-1.

The next stop was Fenway Park in Boston, where Sosa found himself facing All-Star pitcher Roger Clemens. He blew Sammy away with a high fastball in the first inning, but when Clemens faced the Dominican the second time, Sammy hit his first major league home run. And off Roger Clemens, at that! To ice the cake, the Rangers won the game, 10-3.

Sammy was slamming away during the early part of the season, even going 4-for-5 once. But he learned the hard way that you can't count on big-league pitchers to make the same mistakes over again, and they learned to adjust to Sammy.

Sammy Sosa was traded to the Chicago White Sox for right fielder Harold Baines in 1989. During his three years with the White Sox, Sosa hit just .227 with 28 home runs and 113 RBI.

Pretty soon he was seeing nothing but breaking balls, a type of pitch that he had trouble with, and his average fell. Ultimately, he was sent back to the minor leagues. He had played 25 games with the Rangers, during which his batting average fell from .300 to .238. He hit one home run and had three RBI. He was sent to Oklahoma City to play Triple-A ball. He wasn't happy, and his skimpy .103 batting average showed it.

It was in Oklahoma City where he met Larry Himes, general manager of the Chicago White Sox. Despite Sammy's terrible average in Triple-A, Himes decided to bring Sammy to the White Sox by trading the popular Harold Baines for him. Himes explained the unusual trade by saying he saw great potential in Sammy Sosa and that he had been impressed when, after a game in boiling hot Oklahoma City, Sammy went back out on the field and started hitting balls off a batting tee.

OFF TO THE WINDY CITY

Larry Himes said what he saw in Sosa was "a guy with a tremendous arm who could hit between 15 and 20 home runs a year and steal 30 bases. . . . With his speed, we thought he could be a very exciting player."[9] The White Sox sent Sammy to their Triple-A team in Vancouver, British Columbia. In 13 games, he hit .367, and earned a promotion to the big leagues. On August 21, 1989, he donned a White Sox uniform for the first time. The game was against Minnesota in the Metrodome, where Sosa squared off against Twins pitcher Shane Rawley.

Sammy had a good day, taking two walks and hitting two singles, and then, in the ninth inning, he hit his first home run as a White Sock. The Sox won, 10-3. In that season, playing in 33 games, Sosa batted .273 and hit three home runs. But the team was having a terrible year—it finished the season with 69 wins and 92 losses. Only the hapless Detroit Tigers, who dropped 103 games that year, had more losses in the American League.

Sammy was 21 when the 1990 season began, and still a very erratic player. In a game against the California Angels in late June, he got picked off first base, dropped a ball in right field, and then hit a home run to win the game. He was swinging at pitches in the dirt and over his head again. He was throwing the ball over the cutoff man's head, or throwing to the wrong base. Nevertheless, that year he hit 15 home runs, stole more than 30 bases, and had 70 RBI. He also committed 13 errors.

The White Sox had a good year, with 94 wins. That should have been enough to win a pennant, but the Oakland A's, with a hitter named Mark McGwire in the lineup, won 103 games to take the division title. McGwire would, of course, play a large role in Sammy's life in the years to come.

4

Sammy in Chicago

During the 1991 season, Sammy began to have serious problems with the White Sox hitting coach, Walt Hriniak. Hriniak wanted all players to conform to a particular style of batting, and Sammy didn't feel comfortable with that style. His batting suffered as he became more tense and uncomfortable at the plate. His average plunged, and the White Sox sent him back to their Triple-A team in Vancouver. The stay was brief, however, and he was back in the White Sox lineup late in August, in time to play the final games. He was glad when the 1991 season came to an end.

The year wasn't all bad, however. Sammy met Sonia Rodriguez at a nightclub in the Dominican Republic, and they were married. The marriage has been good and the couple have four children: Keysha, Kenia, Sammy Jr., and Michael.

On March 30, as spring training for the 1992 season was about to begin, Sammy was traded across town to the National League Chicago Cubs. The Cubs had hired Sammy's old friend Larry Himes

38

In 1991, Sammy met Sonia Rodriguez at a nightclub in the Dominican Republic and they were married that fall. The couple, who have four children, are pictured here at the eighth annual *GQ* Men of the Year awards in New York, on October 21, 2003.

as general manager. Once again, Himes was the target of much criticism over the trade he made for Sammy. In the trade, he gave up George Bell, the man who was a hero in his native Dominican Republic, who was the Most Valuable Player for the Toronto Blue Jays in 1987, and who had just signed a contract with the Cubs paying him $3 million a year.

Bell was 36 and in the twilight of his career. Himes wanted speed and youth on his team and that's what he felt he would get in Sammy Sosa. He was able to handle the anger of many fans over the trade and the torrent of critical columns in the local papers. Sammy was 23 when the season began. He had to play center field because the right-field job was handled by the great Andre Dawson, who had been the National League's Most Valuable Player in 1987, a year in which he hit 49 home runs and drove in 137 runs.

Sammy hit his first home run as a Cub on May 7. But on June 12, Montreal Expos pitcher Dennis Martinez threw Sammy a tight pitch that hit his right hand, breaking a bone. He was out for six weeks. On his first night back, July 27, he hit a home run against Greg Maddux of the Pittsburgh Pirates before a capacity crowd at Wrigley Field. He then hit two singles and scored the winning run. The Cubs won the second game of the three-game series, and in the final game, Sammy hit another home run in extra innings to win the game.

In nine games after he came off the disabled list, Sammy had a .359 average, hit 3 home runs, scored 8 runs, and had 9 RBI. But in the tenth game after he returned, he hit a ball that caromed off his bat and struck his left ankle. Another bone was broken, and Sammy was out for the rest of the season.

Entering the 1993 season, Sammy had a career total of only 37 home runs. But during the off-season, his salary was raised from $180,000 to $695,000, which was a considerable jump and illustrated how the Cubs' management felt about their future superstar.

THE CURSED CUBS

The Chicago Cubs have played in the same city in the major leagues longer than any other club. The first major league team in Chicago was the White Stockings, established in 1870. The next year, the team became a member of the first professional league—the National Association. That year, the great Chicago fire destroyed the ballpark, uniforms, and club records. The team was out of business for two years because of the fire, but it returned in 1874 and was one of the founding memebers of a new league that replaced the National Association. It was called the National League, as it is today.

In the late 1800s, the White Stockings were among the best teams in the National League. But by the turn of the century, the team had deteriorated into one of the worst. By that time, the team's name had changed to the Chicago Cubs. In the early part of the twentieth century, the Cubs made it to the World Series twice. Their first appearance was in 1907, when they swept Detroit after an opening-game tie. In 1908, the Cubs again made it to the World Series and defeated Detroit in five games. That was the last World Series the club would win.

The Cubs moved to their present ballpark in 1916. It originally was called Weeghman Park, after the team's new owner, Charles Weeghman. It became Wrigley Field in 1926, when William Wrigley, the chewing-gum magnate, bought the team. Over the years, the Cubs had many great stars, including the Hall-of-Fame trio of shortstop Joe Tinker, second baseman Johnny Evers, and first baseman Frank Chance. "Tinker to Evers to Chance" became a kind of mantra when describing the Cubs' great infield in the early twentieth century. Other standouts were pitcher Mordecai "Three Finger" Brown, and another pitcher with the unlikely name of Orval Overall. Sammy Sosa has been compared to Hack Wilson, a Cubs slugger of the 1920s and '30s, whose MLB record 191 RBI in 1930 still stands.

Even with the legendary Leo Durocher as manager, and shortstop Ernie Banks in the lineup in the 1960s, the club still couldn't mount much of a challenge to the league leaders. Affectionately called "Mr. Cub," Banks delighted Wrigley Field fans for years with his sparkling infield play and towering home runs. He had a lifetime total of 512 home runs and was inducted into the National Baseball Hall of Fame in 1977. In 1981, the Wrigley family sold the team to the Chicago Tribune Company, ending their 65-year ownership of the team. Many changes were in store, such as the decision to install lights at Wrigley Field, ending its status as the only major league park where night games couldn't be played. In 1995, the Cubs won their 9,000th game, giving them more wins than any other one-city professional sports franchise. Despite the Cubs' phenomenal history, however, a third World Series win remained out of reach.

TAKING CHANCES

Sammy's speed on the bases helped the team greatly in 1993. The kid who couldn't run the 60-yard dash in less than 7.5 seconds was now getting extra bases because of his speed and effort. In his autobiography, he tells the story of a game against the Phillies that the Cubs were winning, 2-1, on the strength of a Sosa home run. In the sixth inning, with his teammate Derrick May on first, Sammy singled, moving May to second base. Steve Buechele grounded a slow roller to second baseman Mickey Morandini, and it looked like Sammy would be an easy out on his way to second. But he kept running, giving Morandini a head fake and dodging the tag. Instead of being out, he made it into second base and May went on to third. The Phillies screamed that Morandini had tagged him, but the umpire, Larry Vanover, called him safe.

It was that kind of daring that endeared Sammy to the Chicago fans. They never knew what he was going to try to get away with next, and it made for some interesting games. Management was not quite as entertained. "He just needs discipline," his manager, Jim Lefebvre, said. "When he calms down and stays focused, you can see the improvement, but once he starts feeling good about himself, he loses that discipline."[10]

When the season reached the Fourth of July weekend that year, Sammy was red hot. In a Friday night game against the Colorado Rockies in Denver, Sammy had a perfect game—six hits in six at-bats. There were 62,000 fans in Coors Field to witness the feat, which had not been accomplished by a Cub since 1897. Sammy's batting average jumped 19 points, to .284. By that time, he had nine hits in a row, one shy of the National League record. Heading into the last game of the series the next day, Sammy wanted that record, but as an example of his new sense of teamwork, he took a walk instead of chasing a bad pitch, which loaded the bases. Steve Buechele knocked a run home with a sacrifice fly.

Sammy didn't break the record, but sportswriters, who were often critical of Sammy for being a showboat, credited him with a "new maturity" in taking a walk to help the team. He was named National League Player of the Week for the first time. Nobody was happier than General Manager Larry Himes, the man who had made the controversial trade that sent George Bell to the White Sox and brought Sammy to the Cubs. In reference to Sosa, he said, "The only other guy I ever saw with that type of persona, with that type of confidence, was Pete Rose. I played with Pete Rose in the minor leagues, and Pete was the most confident player I had ever been around in my life. Before 1993, Sammy didn't have confidence. But after 1993, it didn't make a difference if he would go 0 for 4. The next day he would be out there trying to beat you."[11]

The "30/30" Club

That September, Sammy achieved another landmark in his career. On September 1, he hit his thirtieth home run. And on September 15, he stole his thirtieth base. He thus became only the tenth player in National League history to achieve the coveted "30/30" mark: 30 home runs and 30 steals in a season. After the game, he picked up the base he had "stolen." He took it home and kept it as a souvenir.

When the season ended, Sammy had 33 home runs and 36 stolen bases. He hit .261 in 598 at-bats. He wasn't proud of his batting average, which was hurt by his 135 strikeouts, but it was a 60-point improvement over the dismal year of 1991. His improvement on the field also allowed him to cash in on a new deal. The Cubs signed him to a $2.95-million, one-year contract. Sammy went out and bought himself a huge gold piece bearing the inscription "30/30" to wear around his neck. "He's got to have the most nerve of anybody I've ever seen," said Larry Himes. "I mean, he's got guts to wear that. But I'm

THE BASEBALL STRIKE OF 1994

What caused the baseball strike of 1994? Money, of course. The players wanted more; the team owners wanted to pay less. Despite long hours and days of negotiations, no agreement could be reached on the major issues: a luxury tax on the big-money teams, revenue sharing to help teams in small-market cities, and a salary cap to hold down the skyrocketing salaries of players.

In other words, it was over who gets the biggest slices of the pie, which is the money made from Major League Baseball, and who was going to be stuck with the smaller pieces? With the average Major League Baseball player making $2.38 million a year, many fans didn't have sympathy with a millionaire going on strike. All many fans saw was that they had to pay more and more for tickets, while neither the owners nor the players seemed to care much about the game.

Gradually, attendance returned to normal, and fans who had given up on baseball drifted back to the game. The restoration of the "national pastime" was helped by the excitement of events like the 1998 home run race between Sammy Sosa and Mark McGwire. "Fortunately, there were some magical moments that reminded people why they liked baseball so much," said pitcher Tom Glavine, who was quoted in an article in the *Cincinnati Enquirer* on August 12, 2004, the 10-year anniversary of the start of the strike.

An agreement was reached in 2002 without any work stoppage, in part because both owners and players feared that another long walkout would destroy baseball altogether. But the issues that divided the owners from the players still exist. And there are those who fear the issues could trigger another strike down the line, possibly when the anger and bitterness of 1994 have faded from memory.

The Chicago Cubs hired former San Diego Padres manager Jim Riggleman in October 1994. Riggleman, who posted a 374–419 record over five seasons with Chicago, is pictured here with famed Cubs broadcaster Harry Caray on the opening day of the season in 1995.

thinking to myself that there was no way this guy was going to let himself be embarrassed."[12]

Sammy played most of 1993 in center field, but when the 1994 season arrived, he was back in right field, where he felt more comfortable. He also established a unique rapport with the right-field fans, always waving to them and cupping his hand to an ear to hear their cheers.

The 1994 season was not one to remember. Not only were the Cubs doing poorly, but also labor unrest was inevitably leading to a crippling strike that would nearly ruin baseball's reputation as the "national pastime." Sammy, however, was doing well. By late July, he was hitting close to .300, had 24 home runs, and 61 RBI. He was looking forward to another 30/30 year and to the record books (only Willie Mays and

Ron Gant posted 30/30 marks in consecutive seasons in National League history), but it was not to be. When the strike began on August 11, Sammy was batting .300, had 25 home runs and 70 RBI, and had stolen 22 bases. There didn't seem to be much doubt that he would have reached 30/30 again, but after 113 games, the season ended.

The strike was over financial issues between the Major League Baseball Players Association and team owners. It became impossible to work out a contract in time to keep the season going. Bud Selig was acting baseball commissioner at the time, and he remembered the agony he went through when he realized he had to call off the season. "I'll never forget the drive home," he said. "After dinner with my wife, I sat in my house and I played over in my mind for hours all the World Series I could remember, starting with 1944. By the time the night was over, I felt even worse. It was unbelievably painful. I remember the hurt, how I felt, how everyone felt."[13]

A NEW START

As the 1995 season began, Larry Himes, Sammy's old friend and mentor, was no longer Cubs general manager, and the team had a new field manager, Jim Riggleman, who came from the San Diego Padres. There was optimism in the Cubs' clubhouse, and the season got off to a good start. The team won its first three games. Sammy was also doing well. By May 22, he was batting .337. In an early season series with the Dodgers, the Cubs were losing, 1-0, when Sammy stepped up to the plate and belted a game-winning home run. What made it a special day was that it was the 9,000th win in the Cubs' history.

Sammy remembers a July 1 game with the St. Louis Cardinals at Wrigley Field, where a record crowd of 39,652 was on hand. By the seventh inning, the Cubs were behind, 7-6. Rey Sanchez led off the inning with a single. Mark Grace also singled and Sammy came up with Sanchez in scoring position. He singled, scoring Sanchez for the tying run. It was Sammy's fourth RBI of the game. Sammy then stole second and scored on a Luis Gonzalez single. It was a game that illus-trated Sammy's new determination to be a team player and not think as much about swinging for the fences. After that game, Sosa got the good news that he would be in the All-Star game for the first time. During the game, which was played in Arlington, Texas, Sammy flied out to left in his one appear-ance at the plate, but he didn't care. He had a great time. "I was honored to be there," he said. "And I'll tell you this, once you play in an All-Star game, you want to go back again. That was my new goal."[14]

In 1995, Sammy was the highest paid player on the Cubs, making $4.3 million. But he was working hard for the money. By late July, he had played in his 116th consecutive game. Unfortunately, the "lovable losers" were not doing well. The good early start did not last. The club went into a slump in mid-season and recovered only when Sammy started pouring it on. In mid-August, he went on a tear, going 6 for 15, and the team started winning again.

In a three-game series in Denver, he hit three home runs: one that traveled 433 feet, another 435 feet, and the longest, 458 feet. By August 20, he was second in the National League in RBI, and the Cubs were winning games. The team began thinking of a wild-card playoff spot. (The "wild card" is awarded to the second-place team with the best record.) Sammy surpassed the record of seven home runs in nine games set by Ryne Sandberg in 1990. He hit seven in seven games.

On August 25, the Atlanta Braves arrived in Chicago for a four-game series. The Cubs' playoff hopes hung in the bal-ance. But the powerful Braves won the first three games. Sosa got only one hit in 10 at-bats and struck out six times. In the fourth game, Sammy hit two home runs, helping the Cubs win, 7-5. Five days later, in a rematch against the Braves in Atlanta, 49,000 people crowded Fulton County Stadium and saw Sammy hit two home runs and drive in four runs in a 6-4 Cubs victory.

ON HIS WAY

In the 1995 season, Sammy passed the 100-RBI mark for the first time in his career, and once again became a 30/30 man. He played in all 144 games (the season had started three weeks late because of the strike), batted .268, hit 36 home runs, and had 119 RBI. Twice in August, he was voted National League Player of the Week. Sammy felt that he had broken through and was on his way to greatness. There were always trade rumors involving Sammy, and they continued as the 1996 season was about to get underway. However, he announced that he wanted to stay in Chicago, especially after the Cubs signed him to a three-year, $16 million contract that January.

By this time, Sammy had homes in Santo Domingo and Chicago, and built a home for his mother in San Pedro de Macoris. His close-knit family often got together in the Dominican Republic and, increasingly, in Chicago. His beloved mother, to whom he continued to give credit for all of his accomplishments, was now financially secure.

During the 1996 season, Sammy started hitting very long home runs. In a game with Cincinnati on April 17, with only 10,023 fans huddled in chilly Wrigley Field, he hit a stunner that wound up on Waveland Avenue, outside the ballpark. The *Chicago Tribune* reported that Sosa "hit a tenth-inning shot that didn't start its descent until local air traffic control gave it clearance." But he also suffered through a slump, not uncommon even for the best ballplayers. At one point, he went 0 for 18. He worked with hitting coach Billy Williams to try to figure out what he was doing wrong, reviewing tapes of his at-bats and taking extra batting practice. He came out of the slump in mid-May, and by May 24, he had 15 home runs, 35 RBI, and 35 runs scored.

Sammy was also getting bigger and stronger. He worked out regularly with weights in his home gym. He was no longer the skinny, malnourished rookie he had once been. He said he could be found working out in his gym as late as 1 A.M. Sammy was also developing into a more complete player. Tommy

LaSorda, manager of the Los Angeles Dodgers, commented, "Sammy Sosa is a five-point player right now. Do you know how many five-point players are in the major leagues? Not many. A five-point player has to hit with power, hit for average, have outstanding speed, have an outstanding arm, and be very good defensively."[15] That was the type of ballplayer Sammy had always wanted to be and had worked so hard to be.

Coming into His Own

By the middle of the 1996 season, Sosa was leading the National League in homers with 23. He had 53 RBI, one of the highest totals in the league. From June 11 through July 18, he put together three 10-game hitting streaks. At the end of July, he was named the National League Most Valuable Player of the Month for the first time in his career. During July, he hit .358 in 26 games, with 22 runs scored, 10 home runs, and 29 RBI. Unfortunately, he was not voted onto the All-Star team. It might have been the first time a player leading the league in home runs didn't make the team. Sammy was hurt, but he tried not to show it.

Then, as if to prove a point, he went on a tear after the All-Star game. Between July 22 and 28, he batted .400, with 4 doubles, 4 home runs, 9 runs scored, and 10 RBI. He was once more named National League Player of the Week. At the same time, the Cubs were losing and that diminished Sammy's pleasure in his own numbers.

During July 1996, Sammy Sosa hit .358, with 22 runs scored, 10 home runs, and 29 RBI on his way to being named the National League Player of the Month. Sosa is pictured here hitting his league-leading thirtieth home run in a 10-5 win over the Pittsburgh Pirates on July 16.

The fans at Wrigley were loyal, however, and continued their loud support of both Sammy and the team.

Manager Jim Riggleman supported Sammy as critics began saying that he was too reckless on the bases and that he never would hit the cutoff man in throws from the outfield: "Well, I've never seen any of that," Riggleman said. "Sure, he makes mistakes. But there seems to be blanket criticism of him. I can't understand why. . . . People are starting to ask me why he's not considered in the same category as Barry Bonds and Ken Griffey. I think he's getting there. I think his time has come. He's one of the elite."[16]

Sammy reached the 40-home run mark with six weeks to go in the season. But his year was about to come to an end. In a game with the Florida Marlins at Wrigley Field, pitcher Mark Hutton threw one in tight and it hit Sammy on the right hand. Sammy thought he would be all right and he kept playing, but the hand swelled and he was in severe pain. It turned out that the ball had broken a bone in his hand. He finished the 1996 season with a .273 batting average, 40 home runs, and 100 RBI. It was his second straight 100-RBI season, despite playing in only 124 games. The Cubs came in fourth place in the National League Central Division with a record of 76 wins and 86 losses.

A DISASTROUS START

Sammy always felt that the 1997 season laid the groundwork for his amazing performance in 1998. "Before 1997 was over, I would experience anxious moments, reevaluate who I was as a player, and come to know things about myself that I hadn't known before," Sosa wrote in his autobiography. Sammy's spirit of giving to the needy may have also started that year when he heard about a program in East Moline, Illinois, where 39 kids and their mentors wanted to come to a Cubs game but couldn't afford it. Sammy invited them to a game as his guests and said later it was one of the few positive moments for him in an otherwise dreary season in which the team dropped its first 14 games.

As was his habit in past seasons, Sammy broke out of a slump of his own in mid-May. Between May 11 and 18, he batted .348, with 4 home runs, 2 triples, and 12 RBI, a career high for him. For the fifth time in his career, he was named National

League Player of the Week. Another milestone came in Pittsburgh on May 26, when he hit his first inside-the-park home run. An inside the parker requires great speed on the bases, and Sammy had it.

On June 27, Sosa signed a four-year, $42.5-million contract with the Cubs, with a $4-million signing bonus. He became the third-highest paid player in the major leagues at that time. He was determined to prove he deserved the money. He played every game and averaged one home run every 17.8 at-bats. Before the end of the year, he hit the 200th home run of his career—and he was just 28 years old. Despite his experience in the majors and the fact that he was one of the top players, Sammy wasn't satisfied. He felt that he still had a lot to learn, especially about hitting.

In mid-season, the Cubs hired Jeff Pentland as hitting coach. He had coached with the New York Mets and the Florida Marlins, and had been power hitter Barry Bonds's college coach at Arizona State. As it turned out, Jeff Pentland would help make 1998 a special season for Sammy Sosa, and pave the way for more records and honors down the line.

As Sammy stated in his autobiography, he was never satisfied with himself, but he never lost his love of the game. "There was a fire inside me to be the best, to excel every time I played," he said. "The reason I played in every game, why I didn't want to sit, was that when game time came around, nobody was more excited than I was. As bad as things were in 1997 for the team, I couldn't wait to get to the park every day and play."

When Jeff Pentland arrived as the hitting coach in 1997, he noticed a few things about Sammy's swing that he thought needed correcting. Sammy was obviously striking out too many times—129 times more than he walked that year, which meant he was still swinging wildly at bad pitches. Pentland said Sammy "had a lot of holes in his swing. You could get him to chase balls if you elevated your pitches. His discipline at the plate was not what it should have been."[17] But he also said

Sammy was open to suggestions, which was crucial in helping him become a better hitter.

MAKING CHANGES

In an interview in 2002, Pentland recalled that Sosa "always seemed like he was in a hurry to hit the ball. Everything was fast and hard and he didn't have much finesse. If you watch boxers, they're always trying to loosen their arms. Relaxation makes you quicker. Tension makes you slow."[18] He convinced Sammy to lower his hands, to utilize his legs as a power source, and, most importantly, to eliminate the "springiness" in his swing. "Power is a matter of coordination, not strength," Pentland said. "The Latin players tend to swing a lot because they want to get over here and participate. The Dominican players are told from a young age: 'You don't get off the island by taking pitches.'"[19]

When Pentland first began to study Sosa's behavior at the plate, he noted that nobody hit the ball harder. "But you just felt like he was out of control all the time. The great hitters can repeat their swing consistently, and they seem to recognize and read balls better than the average player. Sammy wasn't doing that consistently at that time. He was aggressive, but he was wildly aggressive."[20] Pentland thought Sammy was lacking in the crucial ability to read pitches and that was one of the techniques the coach was trying to teach him. What Pentland also saw in Sosa at the end of the disappointing 1997 season was a man who was very unhappy—"even though he was one of the richest players in baseball."[21] Pentland said he decided to try to challenge Sosa to be better.

He told him: "Sammy, your numbers are good, but when are you going to be ready to play in the higher echelon of the game?"

"I don't think he knew any different but to swing for the fences. The important thing about hitting is that it's like opening up a flower. When it's there and the petals are all folded in, you don't know how beautiful it might be. What I made

Sammy aware of was that there was a lot of finesse and softness in hitting."[22]

Here's how Sammy described his work with Jeff Pentland in spring training in Arizona before the legendary 1998 season:

> So we talked about me taking more walks. We talked about me hitting the ball to the opposite field. We talked about hitting over .300. We talked about scoring over 100 runs. We talked technique. We talked game strategies and identifying pitches. We talked about my footwork, where I held the bat, how I held the bat, how I swung the bat. We talked all about hitting.[23]

FALLING LIKE RAIN

Sammy knew what the critics said about him:

* "Sammy Sosa hit 36 home runs, but he struck out 174 times, more than anyone else in the National League."
* "Sammy Sosa drove in 119 RBI, but he hit .246 with men in scoring position, and .159 when pitchers got two strikes on him."
* "Sammy Sosa stole a lot of bases, but he did so in meaningless games and situations. He had a low on-base percentage and made reckless defensive mistakes."[24]

Yes, Sammy knew all that. He had been hearing versions of it for much of his career, not just in 1997. After getting Sammy to lower his arms to get more power into his lower body and legs, Pentland began adjusting his footwork. The style of hitting that Pentland favored was what was called a "tap step." It meant that the hitter moves his front leg toward his back leg as the pitch is on its way. Then he taps it in the dirt before stepping forward as he swings.

Sammy, Pentland observed, was late with the tapping movement. That forced him to hurry his swing. So, the coach came up with a drill in spring training in which Sammy would pull his front foot back, tap, and then pause. Then Pentland would throw him the ball, and he would step forward and hit

Jeff Pentland, whom the Cubs hired in July 1997 to serve as hitting coach for the team, helped Sammy Sosa improve his technique and discipline at the plate. Pentland instructed Sosa to adjust his footwork and lower his arms, so that he could generate more power from his lower body and legs when he swung at a pitch.

it. "We put a pause in there," Pentland said. "Instead of having his feet go back and forth real quick, we changed it. It was *tap back, pause, tap forward*."[25]

Pentland said Sammy picked up the drill immediately. Then they started using a real pitcher in their drills. When the pitcher brought his hands down during his windup, Sammy would tap back. He would train his eye to recognize the pitch. "What came out of the tap step was that Sammy would begin to use his legs better than anybody in the big leagues,"[26] Pentland said.

Jeff Pentland also took on the role of amateur psychologist with Sammy. He insisted that Sammy turn any negative emotions he had into positive ones. He had to overcome all the pettiness that goes on with any ball club. Pentland tried to convince Sammy that a superstar is able to do that. "He had to rise above that part of the game and rise above all the trite little things that were being said in the clubhouse because all that stuff is really meaningless,"[27] Pentland said.

Sammy was happy with the lineup as the 1998 season approached. Fellow Dominican Henry Rodriguez came to the Cubs from the Montreal Expos, where he had a 103-RBI season in 1996 and hit 36 home runs. He would take some of the pressure off Sammy. Rodriguez would play left field, Lance Johnson would play center, and Sammy would be in right field. The club also picked up Mickey Morandini from the Phillies to play second base. Another San Pedro native was Manny Alexander, who would play shortstop. He and Sammy were great friends and confidants. On the mound were Kevin Tapani, Steve Trachsel, and a bright young prospect named Kerry Wood, with Rod Beck in the bullpen.

As the season began, however, the spotlight wasn't on Sammy and the Chicago Cubs. The brightest focus was on Mark McGwire, the St. Louis Cardinals' first baseman. He had hit 58 home runs in 1997, the year in which he was traded to the Cardinals from the Oakland A's. Everywhere "Big Mac" went, reporters asked him the same question: Did he think he could break Roger Maris's record of 61 home runs? Then the spotlight swung toward Seattle, where Ken Griffey Jr. had hit 56 home runs for the Mariners and also seemed to be in the running to surpass Maris's record. He had had five 100-RBI seasons.

As for Sammy, he got off to his usual slow start as the

season began. By mid-May, he was batting only about .200. As Pentland saw it, Sammy's trouble was that he was still hanging on to some of his old habits. Pentland didn't think Sammy was completely sold on the tap-step system. "I felt he was swinging too hard. I wanted to slow him down."[28] So they started a series of drills. Pentland would throw the ball at Sammy underhand from behind a screen and Sammy would practice his stepping. "It's a drill to create a good direction for your swing," Pentland said, "and to keep it slow. I was trying to get him to wait. After a while, he fell in love with what he was learning," Pentland said. "He fell in love with his ability to drive the baseball to right field harder than anybody in the game. When you do something well, you tend to want to do it some more. That's what happened. And once he did that— nobody in baseball could touch him." As Sammy put it, "The home runs came like rain."[29]

6

The History behind 61

Mark McGwire was born on October 1, 1963, two years to the day after Roger Maris broke Babe Ruth's home run record of 60, set in 1927. He was born in Pomona, California, the third of five sons of John and Ginger McGwire. Mark McGwire was an all-round athlete. He played basketball and soccer at Damien High School, a private Catholic boys school. After pulling a muscle in his chest, he switched to golf, and soon excelled at that game. For a time he even thought of becoming a professional golfer. But he returned to baseball, his favorite sport and set his sights on becoming a professional baseball player. Scouts went to see him play in high school and at the University of Southern California, and he eventually signed with the Oakland Athletics in 1984.

The grown-up McGwire was a redheaded giant, but he was basically a shy man who didn't care for the attention he was getting during the 1998 home run race. After Ken Griffey was eliminated and Sammy Sosa became McGwire's leading competitor, the two players hit it off beautifully, despite the fact that their personalities were different. In fact, the high-spirited Sosa was credited with softening the sometimes-edgy McGwire.

The man whose record McGwire and Sosa were chasing was also a shy man who didn't care for the attention he was getting during the 1961 season, when he surpassed Babe Ruth's 60 home runs.

Roger Maris was born in Hibbing, Minnesota, on September 10, 1934. His father, who worked for the Great Northern Railroad, moved the family to North Dakota in 1942. Roger and his older brother, Rudy, played sports and attended Shanley High School in Fargo. The high school did not have a baseball team because of the harsh weather in that part of the country, so Roger played American Legion ball. He led his Legion team to a state championship. Because of his speed, he was an excellent football player as well. In a football game in his senior year, he scored four touchdowns on kickoff returns, setting a national high school record.

The famed coach Bud Wilkinson recruited Roger to play football for the University of Oklahoma, but major league scouts had been after Maris, and he never made it to college. Instead, Maris signed a $15,000 contract to play in the Cleveland Indians' organization. He spent four years in the minor leagues playing for Fargo-Moorhead, Keokuk, Tulsa, Reading, and Indianapolis before making it to the major leagues. He then had outstanding seasons with the Indians and later with the Kansas City Athletics. In 1959, he was elected to the All-Star team.

After the 1959 season, Roger was traded to the New York Yankees. In his first season with the Yankees, he led the major leagues with 27 home runs and 69 RBI halfway through the season. He missed 17 games due to an injury but still led the league with 112 RBI, was second in home runs with 39 (beaten out by his teammate Mickey Mantle, who led the majors with 40), won the Gold Glove award, and was named the American League's Most Valuable Player.

Roger Maris, pictured here in 1962 at Yankee Stadium, broke Babe Ruth's 34-year record for home runs in a season when he hit 62 in 1961. Maris's record stood for 37 years before both Mark McGwire and Sammy Sosa surpassed the mark during the 1998 season.

ROGER MARIS BREAKS THE RECORD

The year 1961 somewhat resembled what happened in 1998. Maris and Mantle were neck and neck as they sought to break Babe Ruth's single-season record of 60 home runs. Maris moved ahead, then Mantle overtook him. No one will ever know who would have won the race, had it continued, because Mantle became ill and missed games at the end of the season. He still finished with a career-high 54 homers.

Maris forged ahead. He tied Ruth on September 26 and then, on October 1, 1961, in the final game of the season, against the Boston Red Sox, Maris hit number 61 off pitcher Tracy Stallard. His home run was the only run, and the Yankees took the game, 1-0. They went on to win the World Series that year, and Roger was named the American League Most Valuable Player for the second consecutive year.

Maris never attained the popularity that the colorful Ruth had with the fans. In fact, there were those who were actually rooting against him. He just didn't have Ruth's charisma. After he hit his 60th home run, critics pointed out that Maris had set his record in 162 games, whereas Ruth attained his in only 154 games. As a result, the league placed an asterisk next to Maris's name in the record books. Eventually, the asterisk was removed and Maris's record became official.

In 1962, Maris hit 33 home runs and drove in 100 runs. He was picked for the All-Star team for the fourth straight year and the Yankees repeated as World Series champs. He missed almost half of the 1963 season with injuries, but still managed to hit 23 home runs and drive in 53 runs. The Yankees went to the World Series again. In 1964, Maris hit 26 home runs and had 71 RBI, and again went to the World Series. Because of injuries, he played in only 46 games for the Yankees in 1965.

He was traded to the St. Louis Cardinals after the 1966 season, and played there his final two years. He helped the Cardinals win the World Series in 1967, when he homered and set a Cardinal record with seven RBI. The Cardinals returned to the World Series the next year and then Maris announced his retirement. In all, he played in seven World Series, hitting six home runs and driving in 18 runs. He finished his career with 275 home runs. Roger Maris died on December 14, 1985, of lymphoma cancer. He was 51.

GEHRIG AND RUTH

Before 1961 and 1998, there was 1927. That year, Babe Ruth and his teammate Lou Gehrig were battling it out for the home

THE BAMBINO

George Herman "Babe" Ruth Jr. was probably the most popular and arguably the most talented baseball player in major league history. He could have had an outstanding career as a pitcher but went on to become a great home run hitter. He was only 19 years old when he started his career with the Boston Red Sox. In the 1916 World Series, he pitched 14 scoreless innings against the old Brooklyn Robins, a record that stands today.

As a pitcher, Ruth posted a career record of 87-44, from 1914 to 1919, and won three World Series games, one in 1916 and two in 1918. At the same time, he was smashing home runs. Because pitchers don't play every game, in 1919 he was switched to the outfield so his hitting prowess could be better utilized. The next year, he was sold to the New York Yankees for $125,000.

He hit the most home runs per season for several years (1919–21, 1923–24, 1926–30) and tied for the home run lead in 1918 and 1931. He set the record of 60 home runs in a season in 1927. He hit a total of 714 home runs in major league play. The record was broken by Hank Aaron, who retired in 1976 with 755.

The Bambino, as he was called, was one of a kind. He certainly didn't look like an athlete. He had a large body and skinny legs, and he kind of minced when he ran around the bases. He also had a flair for the dramatic. In the third game of the World Series against the Chicago Cubs in 1932, he pointed his bat at a spot in the stands in the Cubs' ballpark and promptly hit a home run there. The Babe and his teammate Lou Gehrig visited sick children in hospitals and promised to hit home runs for them. And they usually delivered.

In 1935, he was traded to the National League's Boston Braves, where he finished his career. Before he died of cancer in 1948, he endowed the Babe Ruth Foundation to aid underprivileged children. In 1936, he became the second man inducted into the Hall of Fame. The first was the legendary Detroit Tigers' centerfielder, Ty Cobb.

run crown. Gehrig went through a slump in September and finished the season with 47 home runs. Ruth, by contrast, had a great September. He hit 17 home runs that month and got his 60th in the final game of the season.

Babe Ruth, born George Herman Ruth Jr., started his base-ball career as a pitcher. He pitched for the Boston Red Sox before being traded to the Yankees in 1920. He then became an outfielder and belted a record 54 home runs. The closest American Leaguer was George Sisler, who had just 19. When Babe hit 59 the following year, he was in a class by himself. His nearest rival hit only 24.

There were some great sluggers in the 1930s. Jimmie Foxx hit 58 home runs in 1932, and Hank Greenberg recorded the same number in 1938. But the emphasis in baseball was not on hitting home runs. Rather, it was a game of strategy, where it was more important for a batter to find a way to get on base, whether with a single or a walk, and advance runners with sacrifice bunts or flies, stolen bases, or whatever it took to get the runs in. The home run was a special treat for the fans. While the big hitters could pull in the fans, they did not always help their teams that much, as Sammy Sosa's story illustrates.

DARING TO DREAM

Roger Maris's home run record of 61 had stood for nearly four decades. No one had come even close to it in all that time. It seemed like the impossible dream. But three men in 1998 dared to dream.

At the beginning of the season, Mark McGwire of the St. Louis Cardinals and Ken Griffey Jr. of the Seattle Mariners were the leading contenders. McGwire had hit 58 home runs in 1997 and Griffey had hit 56. Sosa, who was not thought of as a serious threat until mid-season, came off a 36-home run season, in which he also led the National League in strikeouts with 174. That didn't stop Sosa from thinking about the record. In fact, when asked by a reporter at the beginning of the 1997 season if he could hit 50 home runs that year, he had replied, "Why not 60?"

Mark McGwire started off the 1998 season with a grand slam home run in the Cardinals' first game, and followed that with home runs in the next three games. By the end of April, McGwire and Ken Griffey had hit 11 home runs each. The Cubs, meanwhile, were doing well. Compared to the previous season, when the team lost its first 14 games, the 1998 squad reeled off six straight victories after dropping the opener. More crucial to the club's success than anything Sammy Sosa was doing was the strong pitching the Cubs were getting from starters Mark Clark, Kevin Tapani, and Steve Trachsel, and from closer Rod Beck. In addition, the team had a young pitching phenomenon in 20-year-old Kerry Wood. In fact, Wood, a 6-foot-5, 225-pound powerhouse, was doing so well that he cornered the press coverage.

DAILY WORKOUTS

Sammy was hitting well, even if he wasn't popping a lot of homers. He was being more selective at the plate, and he and hitting coach Jeff Pentland were working daily on his stance and swing. Pentland would lob the ball to Sammy, causing Sammy to wait on the pitch and try to overcome his wild, free-swinging ways. The drill was also aimed at getting Sammy to hit to right field, called the "opposite field" in baseball lingo. That's because a right-handed hitter like Sosa naturally hits the ball to left field, where the fielders expect him to hit the ball. By learning to hit to the opposite field, a hitter has a better chance of getting a hit.

By the end of April, the Cubs were enduring their first slump and were just a game over the .500 mark, at 14 wins, 13 losses. At that time, Sammy had six home runs. Cubs Rookie Kerry Wood started making headlines when he pitched a one-hit shutout against the Houston Astros in his fourth major league start. He struck out 20 hitters, tying the major league record set by Roger Clemens in 1987. Only three other pitchers

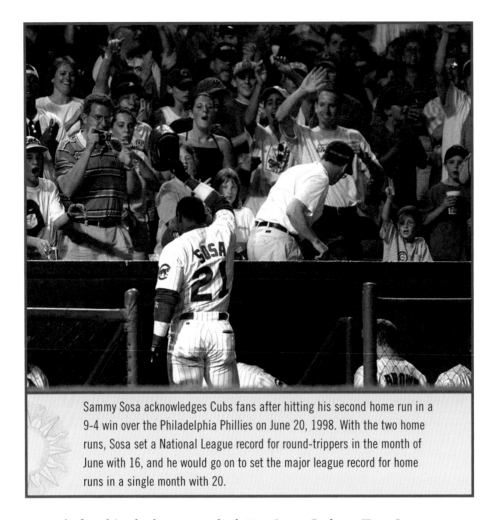

Sammy Sosa acknowledges Cubs fans after hitting his second home run in a 9-4 win over the Philadelphia Phillies on June 20, 1998. With the two home runs, Sosa set a National League record for round-trippers in the month of June with 16, and he would go on to set the major league record for home runs in a single month with 20.

before him had even reached 19—Steve Carlton, Tom Seaver, and David Cone. Reporters rushed to Chicago to write about Wood, then dashed to New York, where David Wells pitched just the fifteenth perfect game in major league history, beating the Minnesota Twins, 4-0.

Around this time, Mark McGwire began blasting long home runs in bunches: he hit one 527 feet against the Brewers and another 545 feet against the Florida Marlins. He hit 12 homers between May 12 and May 25, including three in a game at Philadelphia on May 25. By the end of May, Big Mac (as McGwire was called) had 27 home runs and Griffey had 19. Sammy Sosa, in contrast, had a mere 13.

Sammy was concentrating on being a more disciplined hitter, which some believed hurt his ability to hit home runs. He wasn't taking those wild swings that could either send the ball over the wall or lead to another strikeout. Jeff Blauser, a veteran shortstop who was new to the Cubs that year, made an interesting observation when he watched Sosa at the plate. "I think there comes a time in every player's career when he plays for the team and doesn't worry anymore about getting established or putting up numbers,"[30] he said. Nevertheless, Sammy was about to embark on a June to remember.

Sosa hit two homers against the Florida Marlins at Wrigley on June 1, another one on June 3, then another on June 6, and another on June 8. That round-tripper helped give the Cubs their tenth straight win. Now Sammy had homered in four straight games and his season total had reached 20. Suddenly, he was only nine homers behind Big Mac. But Sammy was just getting warmed up. He went four days without a homer then hit one on June 13 at Philadelphia. He slammed three more in a game against Milwaukee at Wrigley two days later. He hit another on June 17, then two against the Phillies on June 19, and two more against the Phillies the next day.

COMING ON STRONG

Sportswriters around the country were beginning to notice Sosa. When Sammy hit a solo shot on June 21, he had reached 17 for the month, making 30 for the year, and was only three home runs behind McGwire. In addition, Sammy was heading for another record. Back in August 1937, a slugger named Rudy York set a major league record by hitting 18 home runs in the month of August for the Detroit Tigers.

Sammy's manager, perhaps thinking about the hulking McGwire, said, "You don't have to be a big man to hit the ball hard and hit the ball a long way."[31] He noted that what it takes is timing and making contact with the ball at the right spot. After ten years in the majors, Sammy Sosa seemed at last to have learned how to hit. Sammy was named National League

Player of the Week for June 15 to 21. He led the league in homers, RBI, total bases, hits, slugging percentage, and runs scored. He went 13 for 30 (.433). Sammy himself saw the difference in his approach to hitting. "I just have in my mind to go up there, make contact, and go to right field. Last year, I was in a situation where I was swinging at every pitch. This year I have a different attitude."[32]

7

The Race Is On

On June 24, Sammy hit his eighteenth home run for the month at Detroit, matching Rudy York's record. The next night in Detroit, batting against Brian Moehler in the seventh inning, he broke York's record by hitting his nineteenth homer for June. Then on June 30, he smacked homer number 33 and his twentieth in June against the Arizona Diamondbacks at Wrigley Field.

Sammy's 33 home runs at the end of June had tied him with Griffey. McGwire had 37 at that point. Reporters persisted in asking him if he thought he could catch Mark McGwire and reach Roger Maris's record. Sammy would consistently reply with something like, "Mark McGwire is in a different world. He's my idol. He's the man. I have a lot of respect for that guy."[33] He also deflected questions about Roger Maris. "No, no, no. That guy's a legend. I just want to continue the way I am and do the little things for my team to win the games, and whatever happens happens."[34]

After his spectacular June, Sammy was invited to the All-Star game. He was looking forward to participating in the home run hitting contest preceding the All-Star game and playing in the game itself. But he did not participate in either that year, because of a sore left shoulder, which he said might have been caused by sleeping awkwardly on it. Heading into the All-Star break, the Cubs had 48 wins and 39 losses and were in a good position to make the playoffs, at least as a wild-card team.

The pressure of the home run competition was beginning to get to McGwire, a guy who was never comfortable in the public eye. He said he was feeling like a "caged animal." And Griffey had made it clear he wasn't going to answer any more questions about the contest. Only Sammy, with his ready smile and outgoing personality, still gave interviews, signed autographs, and seemed to be having a great time through it all.

Cubs coach Billy Williams realized that the reason Sosa could keep everything in perspective was because of where he came from. He said the attention was easy for Sammy. "Shining shoes, that was the pressure. He kind of looks at things in a different way than other players. He's a person who is at peace with himself. And when you're at peace with yourself, you can handle a lot of stuff."[35]

By the end of July, McGwire had 45 home runs, Sosa had 42, and Griffey, 41. Earlier in the month, *Time* magazine did a cover story on the home run race, with photos of McGwire and Griffey on the cover. Inside was a story about Sammy that read in part: "Sosa is the dark-horse candidate to shatter the single-season record for home runs. Thanks to a spectacular—some might say freaky—June in which he popped 20 home runs, a major league record, the Dominican native showed that he is finally harnessing his impulsiveness." Sammy liked the headline, which read: "Hey Guys, Watch Your Backs—Here Comes Sammy!"

INTO THE SUMMER

The Cubs were doing well in 1998 partly because they had other players besides Sosa to carry the team. At the end of July,

the Cubs had a 62-48 record. The team had no chance of winning the Central Division, however. The Houston Astros
appeared to have that wrapped up, especially after they traded
for All-Star pitcher Randy Johnson. At the same time,
McGwire's Cardinals and Griffey's Mariners were out of the
race for playoff spots. Their premier home run hitters couldn't
save their teams either.

When August and the summer heat arrived, there was
speculation that the hitters would slow down. Not so. Sammy
and Big Mac continued blazing away. It was Griffey who faltered. He started slipping farther behind the leaders. By August
18, the race was tied. Sosa and McGwire were knotted with 47
homers apiece.

During the race, McGwire and Sosa frequently met on the
field. They seemed to be the best of friends. They laughed a lot
together. Sammy said he wanted two things out of the 1998
season—for McGwire to beat Roger Maris's record and for the
Cubs to make the playoffs. McGwire was still his idol. He was
"the man," Sammy insisted.

Before a game between the Cardinals and Cubs, Sammy
went up to McGwire, who was on the ground doing stretching
exercises. McGwire barked, "Get away! Get away!" and everyone thought the race had finally gotten to his nerves. But then
he laughed, jumped up, and gave Sammy a bear hug. Sammy
actually had some advice for his rival. "Sometimes I see that he
is trying too hard to hit a home run," he said. "Sometimes I
wish he would relax more at the plate."[36] But belting record
numbers of home runs was not new to McGwire. At that point,
he was one of two players in baseball history to hit 50 or more
home runs for two years in a row: 52 in 1996 and 58 in 1997.
On August 20, 1998, he hit number 50, and he alone held the
record of hitting 50 or more home runs for three years running.

Sammy hit eight homers from August 19 to 31, including
two in a game against Houston. He ended the month with 55,
tied with McGwire. Big Mac had a couple of two-homer
games, one against the Cubs on the nineteenth, in which

Sammy hit one, and against the Mets the next day. He reached 55 with a homer against the Braves on August 30.

Baseball was making big money from the home run contest. Attendance was up 3 percent, and several teams went over the 2-million attendance total for the season. It looked like the bitterness from the 1994 strike had come to an end.

In Latin America, Sammy was hailed as a credit to his origins. In San Pedro de Macoris, as in much of Central and South America, the streets were eerily quiet and deserted when a Cubs game was on TV.

THE RECORD FALLS

When September arrived, McGwire took off. He hit a pair of homers against the Marlins in Florida on the first day of the month, and then followed up with two more the next day. He had surpassed Hack Wilson's National League record of 56 home runs in a season. Sammy hit a homer against Cincinnati on September 2, giving him 56 and a tie with Hack Wilson. On September 4, in a game at Pittsburgh, Sammy moved past Hack Wilson's 56 with a shot off Jason Schmidt in the first inning. More important to Sammy, however, was the fact that the Cubs won the game and ran their season record to 80 wins and 62 losses. The team was fighting it out with the Mets for the wild-card berth.

Mark McGwire hit his sixtieth home run on September 5 against the Cincinnati Reds at Busch Stadium, tying the Babe's record. The same day, Sammy hit his fifty-eighth at Pittsburgh. After a day off, the Cards and Cubs would be meeting for a two-game series at Busch Stadium. Sammy and Big Mac would be going head-to-head.

It was obvious from their several meetings with the press prior to that series that the two had no personal animosity toward each other. In fact, each said he was rooting for the other. "I am a fan of the game, as well as a player," McGwire said at one joint press conference. "[Sammy] is having an absolutely magical year and, you know, I root him on just

Sammy Sosa and Mark McGwire enjoy a lighter moment during their joint press conference prior to the Cubs-Cardinals game on September 7, 1998. McGwire tied Roger Maris's home run record in game one of the series, a 3-2 Cardinals win, and broke the record in the Cardinals' 6-3 win in game two.

like anybody else. Wouldn't it be great if we just ended up tied?"[37]

It was a Monday night, September 7, when the first game began. Veteran right-hander Mike Morgan was on the mound for the Cubs. In the first inning, Big Mac sent a Mike Morgan fastball 430 feet into the left-field stands for his sixty-first home run. He had tied Roger Maris's record. In the stands were five of Maris's six children, and McGwire saluted them as he crossed the plate. Roger's widow had been hospitalized with a rapid heartbeat and couldn't attend. Also in the stands were McGwire's parents, and McGwire's son Matt was serving as the

Cards' batboy. Mark picked him up and gave him a hug. He also waved at Sammy, who was in right field applauding. Sammy got only one hit in five at-bats and the Cardinals won, 3-2.

The second game attracted even more attention from the press and baseball fans around the world. McGwire had a chance to break the 37-year-old home run record. In the fourth inning, McGwire took a pitch from right-hander Steve Trachsel and drove it down the left-field line, where it just cleared the wall. It was a line drive, and at 341 feet, one of McGwire's shortest homers. But it was enough to shatter Maris's record, and the jammed stadium erupted.

As he ran around the bases, McGwire high-fived and hugged Cubs infielders, who seemed as happy as he was about the record-breaker. He again scooped up his son, waved to his parents, and then turned to where the Maris children were sitting in the stands. He touched his heart and pointed to the sky. Sammy then came in from right field and the two sluggers embraced. At a press conference afterward, a smiling Sammy Sosa repeated how good he felt for his friend. But he had to have been disappointed that his team again lost, 6-3. Sammy revealed at the press conference that when he was on first base later in the game, he said to Mac, "Congratulations. Now don't go too far. Wait for me."

It was interesting to note that both Babe Ruth and Roger Maris set their records in the final game of the season. But McGwire had broken Maris's record with 18 games left to play. At that point, Sammy had 58 homers. Sammy closed the distance between them on Friday, September 11, when he hit his fifty-ninth homer against the Milwaukee Brewers at Wrigley. Unfortunately, his team lost, 13-11.

The next day, Sammy clobbered his sixtieth four-bagger against Valerio De Los Santos of Milwaukee at Wrigley. It was another blast that landed in Waveland Avenue outside the park. He was proud of the fact that he was only the fourth player in baseball history to hit 60 or more home runs in a season, and the first Latin American to do so. And even better, the

THE ECONOMICS OF THE HOME RUN RACE

The home run race in 1998 between the Cardinals' Mark McGwire and the Chicago Cubs' Sammy Sosa is credited with restoring baseball, badly damaged by the crippling strike of 1994, as the "national pastime." It also made some people a lot of money.

The man who caught Mark McGwire's seventieth home run in 1998 was a St. Louis Cardinals fan named Philip Ozersky. On September 27, 1998, McGwire hit a drive that soared over the left-field wall at Busch Stadium, bounced underneath a set of metal bleachers, and hopped into Ozersky's waiting hands. Ozersky knew he had a piece of history, a valuable prize to commemorate one of the most remarkable seasons in Major League Baseball history. He sold it for $2.7 million, paid $1.2 million in taxes, donated about $250,000 to charity, and bought a caricature of McGwire for $10,000.

As reported in the *New York Times* on March 15, 2005, the *St. Louis Post-Dispatch* published 500,000 extra copies the day after McGwire broke Roger Maris's record of 61 home runs on September 8. They sold every copy.

Television also enjoyed a boost in ratings: The Fox network's numbers were up 11 percent, and Major League Baseball estimated it made $1.5 billion in television revenue from the home run race.

Even a restaurant called the Abbey, in Seal Beach, California, gained a measure of fame and fortune when McGwire, a frequent patron, wore baseball caps with "The Abbey" emblazoned on them during press conferences. "It made business boom," the *Times* quoted the owner, Mike Burdick, as saying. "People would come in here and just want to be part of the chase."

For his part, McGwire didn't like all the attention. About 500 reporters followed him just about everywhere he went. He had one favorite "reporter," though, a ten-year-old boy who asked questions like, "Who could eat more hot dogs, you or Babe Ruth?"

Cubs won, 15-12, giving them an 83-66 record and keeping them apace with the Mets for that wild-card playoff spot.

Jeff Pentland, the coach who had helped Sammy change his approach to hitting, said he was so overcome on the day Sammy hit his sixtieth home run, he had to go back into the tunnel on the way to the clubhouse to be alone with his emotions. "In my mind, 60 had always been a magical number, and at that moment everything just kind of hit me. After a while, I just couldn't hold back my tears, and I just lost it. Who was I? Where did I come from? I was a nobody, and here I was a part of history. It was overwhelming to me."[38]

LOVE LETTER

On Sunday, September 13, Mark McGwire had to leave a game with the Astros with back spasms. That day, in another game with the Brewers, Sammy popped one over the left-field wall off Bronswell Patrick. He had tied Maris's record, but he wasn't finished. In the ninth inning, trailing the Brewers by a run, Sammy hit an Eric Plunk fastball 480 feet over the wall at almost the same spot in left field. He had tied McGwire at 62. Crazed fans demanded three curtain calls from their hero. Sammy's shot had tied the game, and the Cubs went on to win, 11-10, when Mark Grace hit a two-out homer in the tenth inning. "It's hard to describe the emotions I was feeling as I ran around the bases," Sammy wrote in his autobiography. "I had wanted this so much, and now I had achieved it. Everything had come to me, everything I had ever dreamed of, and now I was rounding the bases as a part of history."

He sent a message to McGwire, saying, "Mark, you know I love you. It's been unbelievable. I wish you could be here with me today. I know you are watching me and I know you have the same feeling for me as I have for you in my heart."[39] A newspaper reporter in the Dominican Republic said, "We all feel as if we had hit that home run ourselves."[40]

Sammy was on the cover of *Sports Illustrated*, and ESPN did an hour interview with him. The season had yet another distinction, however. Ken Griffey Jr. finished his season with 52 home runs, and 1998 became the first in which three players hit 50 or more.

THE GREAT MOMENT

Despite tenderness in his back, McGwire pinch-hit on September 15 and belted a home run against Pittsburgh at Busch Stadium for his sixty-third. There seemed to be no end to his amazing productivity. On September 16, the Cubs were playing a three-game series against the Padres in San Diego. The Padres were leading the National League West, and they took the first two games against the Cubs. In the third game, the Padres were leading by a 2-0 score when Sammy came up with the bases loaded. He hit a double into the left-field corner to drive in the tying run. The game was still tied in the eighth when the Cubs loaded the bases once more. That set up the moment that writer Marcos Breton described as one of his greatest experiences as a sports reporter for the *Sacramento Bee*.

Pitcher Brian Boehringer was on the mound for the Padres. There were two outs. Sammy swung at a couple of pitches, and each time he missed, the crowd groaned. This was a San Diego crowd, but they were cheering for a Cub! Breton described what happened when Boehringer hung a pitch over the plate:

> I'll never forget that moment. I was standing in the left-field bleachers and I saw Sosa follow through against a backdrop of flashing lights. When he connected, the thousands of people in the sections in front of me seemed to move as one. Then the screams of the crowd grew louder and louder as the ball sailed toward the bleachers.
>
> Before I knew it, the ball was soaring over me, over all the people in the lower pavilion and into the second deck—434 feet from home plate.
>
> A grand slam! Home run number 63.

At a press conference prior to the Chicago Cubs' game against the San Diego Padres on September 17, Sammy Sosa holds up the baseball he hit to reach 63 home runs in the 1998 season. Fabian Perez Mercado, who caught the home run ball, and his son, Carlos, congratulate Sosa on his accomplishment.

Despite the fact that Sosa was a visiting player, fireworks exploded throughout the stadium. And the crowd wouldn't stop cheering until Sosa emerged from the Cubs' dugout to take a bow. Some of the Padres' players appeared unhappy with the display, which saddened Sammy. It wasn't so much him they were applauding, he said. "What people were responding to was history,"[41] he said. At that point, Sammy was once again tied with McGwire and had 154 RBI, the highest total in the major leagues in 1998.

8

Sammy in the Community

On September 20, Sammy was honored at a "Sammy Sosa Celebration" at Wrigley Field. Major League Baseball Commissioner Bud Selig was on hand, as were Sammy's wife and mother. Chicago Bulls basketball star Michael Jordan, one of Sammy's heroes, was there to pay homage to the great season Sammy was having.

About this time, McGwire was answering a lot of questions about his use of androstenedione, called "andro" among users. And reporters started asking Sosa about andro because he and McGwire had become linked in the home run race. Sammy told reporters what McGwire did was his business. In his autobiography, Sammy commented, "I can only speak for myself. And I have never used andro, nor do I plan to. By 1998, my upper body had developed significantly from my first year in the majors, when I was a skinny 20-year-old from San Pedro. While it's true that I tried the food supplement creatine once or twice, I never saw it have any particular impact on my body or development. The truth is, I attributed my

Sammy Sosa tips his cap to Cubs fans during "Sammy Sosa Day," which was held at Chicago's Wrigley Field on September 20, 1998, to honor the Dominican slugger. Despite losing the game to the Cincinnati Reds, 7-3, Sosa was able to share the special day with his family, who were flown in from the Dominican Republic.

physical development to many years of strict weight training and proper nutrition."[42]

The Cubs were still in contention for the 1998 playoffs. After losing three games, the team rebounded by beating the Brewers, 5-2. After going hitless in 21 at-bats, Sammy made a dramatic comeback from his slump. Against the Brewers on September 23 in Milwaukee, he hit two home runs, his sixty-fourth and sixty-fifth, and once again tied Mighty Mac. Unfortunately, the Cubs blew a 7-0 lead and lost the game, 8-7.

There were only three games left in what would go down in baseball history as one of the greatest and most exciting seasons ever. But the thrills weren't over yet. The Cubs were vying with the Mets and the Giants for the wild-card spot when the Cubs went up against the National League Central Division champs, the Houston Astros, in the Astrodome in Houston. Sammy was facing a fellow Dominican, Jose Lima, when he launched a 462-foot bomb in the fourth inning—his sixty-sixth home run and his last four-bagger of the amazing season. But McGwire wasn't about to stop. Word came from St. Louis that McGwire had blasted his sixty-sixth against Montreal.

At that point, Sammy was becoming increasingly concerned about the devastation that Hurricane Georges had wreaked on the Dominican Republic, especially his home city of San Pedro de Macoris. He would discover later that his accomplishments on the ball fields of the United States actually helped the home folk survive. As the tons of food, clothing, and medicine that the Sammy Sosa Charitable Foundation, and many other relief organizations, were in the process of being shipped to the battered country, a local priest, the Reverend Torivio Rodriguez, said, "Sammy is giving these people something to look forward to. He's clearly a source of inspiration and hope throughout the city."[43]

ONE-GAME PLAYOFF

In the United States, Sammy insisted that he was more concerned with helping to win a playoff spot for the Cubs than accumulating home runs. The Cubs got a break when the Giants lost their final game, setting up a one-game playoff between the Cubs and the Giants. The game was played at Wrigley, and Sammy's friend Michael Jordan, the Chicago Bulls' great player, threw out the first pitch. Sammy failed to get a hit his first two times at bat and the game was scoreless heading into the fifth inning. Then Gary Gaetti hit a two-run homer to give the Cubs a 2-0 lead. In the sixth, Lance Johnson singled and Sammy followed with a single. Both eventually scored on a Matt Mieske single. The Cubs were up, 4-0. After Sammy's single, former Cincinnati star Joe Morgan, who was broadcasting the game, commented, "Many people don't believe that Sammy doesn't always swing for home runs. But I've seen several situations in the past weeks when he's shortened his swing and singled because that was best for his team. He truly is a team player."[44]

In Sammy's final at-bat of the game, he hit another single and eventually scored on a wild pitch. The Cubs' lead was extended to 5-0. The Giants scored three runs in the ninth inning, but Rod Beck shut them down and the Cubs won the game, 5-3, to go to the playoffs. Sammy celebrated by climbing to the roof of the dugout and doing the merengue, the national dance of the Dominican Republic.

The Cubs were knocked out of the playoffs by the Atlanta Braves, but Sammy had put together a remarkable season. He finished the year with a batting average of .308, 66 homers, a major league-leading 158 RBI, and 134 runs scored, which also led the league. He was named the National League Most Valuable Player. Mark McGwire had gone on a hot streak and hit two home runs in each of his final two games, reaching 70 for the season.

HELPING THE KIDS

In the aftermath of the 1998 season, Sammy received a stream of praise and awards. Mark McGwire and he were named "Sportsmen of the Year" by *Sports Illustrated* and the *Sporting News*. Sammy was in the Capitol during President Clinton's State of the Union address and got a standing ovation from Congress when Clinton introduced him. He met celebrities from Hollywood and politicians and government leaders. The Dominican Republic community in New York threw a big parade for Sammy and he returned to his native land a national hero. "When I arrived home, people lined the streets," he wrote in his autobiography. "You could still see the damage from the hurricane, and it rained very, very hard—but still the people were there by the thousands. It touched my heart to see them all, to know they had waited for me in the rain. I'll never forget that day."

In 1998, before Hurricane Georges hit, he founded the Sammy Sosa Foundation in order to raise funds for underprivileged children in both Chicago and the Dominican Republic. In the aftermath of the hurricane, the foundation provided food, clothing, and medical supplies to the country. Sosa also encouraged contributions from business firms, charitable organizations, and individuals. Mark McGwire, his home run competitor, chipped in $100,000. In 1999, Sosa's foundation later opened the Sammy Sosa Children's Medical Center for Preventive Medicine in San Pedro, with the help of the U.S. Centers for Disease Control and Prevention in Atlanta, and the U.S. and Dominican governments. The clinic provides free immunizations to children in the five provinces surrounding San Pedro. For his humanitarian efforts, Sammy was presented with the Roberto Clemente Man of the Year award by Major League Baseball. It was a special honor for him because Clemente was one of his heroes.

Clemente, the Hall of Fame outfielder for the Pittsburgh Pirates who was born in Puerto Rico, won four National League batting titles and helped the Pirates win two World Series championships. He was the National League's Most Valuable Player in 1966, and the Most Valuable Player in the 1971 World Series. At the age of 38, he collected the 3,000th hit of his career in his last at-bat of the season. Clemente was also a great humanitarian who planned to build a sports city in Puerto Rico for youngsters starting their careers in athletics.

On December 23, 1972, a devastating earthquake tore through Nicaragua. On New Year's Eve, Clemente boarded a plane loaded with medical and food supplies for the victims. The plane crashed at sea, killing all aboard. Sammy would proudly wear Clemente's number 21 on his uniform after he arrived in the major leagues and has worn it throughout his playing career.

SAMMY SUNDAYS
The centerpiece of Sammy's charitable activities in the
(continued on page 86)

SAMMY SOSA'S LOVE
OF THE DOMINICAN REPUBLIC

Despite Sammy Sosa's great successes on the baseball field and as a humanitarian, and despite the millions he has made with his skills on the diamond, he has never forgotten where he came from and how much he owes to his homeland of the Dominican Republic, its people, and his family who still live there.

In his autobiography, Sammy relates a journey he loved to make during the off-season, when he would travel from his home in Santo Domingo to where he grew up, the city of San Pedro de Macoris. It is a town of 200,000 people that has sent far more than its share of baseball players to the American big leagues.

Sammy calls it the "city of hope," because that's where the kids grow up as he did dreaming of the gleaming baseball fields of the United States. Whenever he goes home to San Pedro, Sammy takes a journey back through the memories of his childhood, back to where he learned to play baseball on a rock-strewn playground not far from where he grew up in the same poverty that is still endemic to the city. He wrote in his autobiography that he makes this trip "to remind myself of where I came from, of what gives me strength, of what made me who I am. And every time I make it, the journey becomes a kind of celebration—not of home runs or millions of dollars, but of faith.

In fact, my life is a celebration of faith—faith in my abilities as a baseball player when no team wanted me, of my faith in God when my family and I were hungry and penniless. And faith in the most important, most cherished person in my life: my blessed mother, Mireya."*

Sammy is truly a people person. He enjoys nothing more than meeting with his fellow Dominicans, especially the kids who look up to him and yearn to be like him someday. He goes to the playground with his uniform, his bats and gloves, and works out as the townsfolk and the kids rush to greet him:

As we approach the small playground in San Pedro, I'm transported back in time. Whenever my vehicle pulls up, it provides quite a contrast to the humble surroundings. Bumping along a dirt road that leads to a ragged baseball diamond with no infield grass, I witness the same scene each time I come here. Running along each side of my vehicle are young children dressed in stained T-shirts and cut-off shorts. Some shout my name, "Sammy! Sammy!"**

. . . Here in San Pedro, I work out hard no matter how many kids show up, no matter how many adults compete for my attention, tell me their problems, ask for help, or try to get me interested in some idea or some detail they just have to share with me. This is who I am—I love being around people.***

And Sammy gets a big kick out of watching the kids work out, reminding him of how hard he worked at their age to make it to the United States. "After taking my hacks," he wrote, "I love to sit on a chair very near home plate and watch the local kids, eagerly dressed in baseball uniforms that dangle off their skinny frames, as they take batting practice. I smile as young pitchers and catchers throw that little bit extra into what they are doing, showing off for me. I offer words of encouragement to these kids because for a lot of my youth, encouragement was in very short supply."†

A lot of people who come from humble beginnings and attain great things in their life might not want to remember where they came from, but it seems that Sammy has no inclination to forget what he owes his country and its people.

"There is great poverty in my country," he wrote, "and it surrounds this park. I used to shine shoes near here. I used to live near here, in a one-bedroom house with dirt floors and no indoor plumbing.

Those kinds of dwellings have not disappeared with the passage of time. The people who are always waiting for me at the park in San Pedro live that way today. These are my people."††

* Sammy Sosa, *Sosa: An Autobiography* (New York: Warner Books, 2000), 14.

** Ibid., 15.

*** Ibid., 17.

† Ibid., 18.

†† Ibid., 16.

(*continued from page 83*)

Dominican Republic, the Children's Medical Center for Preventive Medicine in San Pedro, is located in Sosa's 30/30 Plaza, the name of which commemorates his record of reaching more than 30 home runs and 30 stolen bases in two seasons. In the middle of the mall is a fountain with a statue of Sosa in his Cubs uniform. The fountain is dedicated to shoeshine boys, which he once was, and bears the inscription: "The coins thrown in here go to charity."

Sammy also provided business space for two sisters, Raquel, who ran a beauty salon, and Sonia, who had a clothing boutique. He purchased a number of ambulances to improve emergency medical care in the Dominican Republic, and, during his 1998 season, donated 40 computers to schools there for each home run he hit. In Chicago, he devoted time to the Wyler Children's Hospital, and staged what he called "Sammy Sosa Sundays" at Wrigley Field, inviting kids who couldn't afford to attend games to be his guest.

However, *Fortune* magazine reported in a lengthy article in its April 17, 2000, issue that the Sosa foundation was a financial mess. The magazine said the foundation was "broke and in disarray." Bill Chase, the factory owner who had befriended Sosa when he was a teenager and gave him his first baseball glove, was president of the foundation. He defended it against *Fortune's* allegations. By August 2000, most of the problems had been resolved. Sosa hired a California lawyer named Roger Browning to straighten it out. The conclusion by Daniel Sterner, a Florida assistant attorney general who led an investigation of the charity, was that the operators were well intentioned, but "clearly over their heads." In other words, there were no illegalities, and Sosa compensated the foundation for funds spent on questionable activities. "Most of our questions appear to be answered,"[45] Sterner said.

ANOTHER RECORD.

In the 1999 season, Sammy Sosa and Mark McGwire engaged in another home run race, but it wasn't the same. The press and the public didn't seem as excited. After all, it was old news, and the American public has always had a short attention span. Sammy hit 63 home runs that year and McGwire 65. In any other year, this would have been a huge accomplishment.

The Cubs were another story. The team lost 95 games in one of its worst seasons. It was especially painful because the team had been good enough to make the playoffs the year before. Despite this, 1999 was one of Sammy's best. He batted .288 and had 158 RBI, in addition to his home runs. He was proud of the fact that he hit his sixty-third home run in St. Louis with the president of the Dominican Republic in the stands. "I think Sammy had a better year in 1999 than he did in 1998," Jeff Pentland, his hitting coach, said. "To me, what was great about 1999 was Sammy was now consistently hitting the best pitchers in the game. Now he was able to hit well against Randy Johnson, Kevin Brown, and Curt Schilling. You could go down the list, and Sammy hit off them. That was special."[46] Sammy was also proud of the fact that the fans voted him into the starting lineup of the All-Star game for the first time. He was the leading vote getter in baseball, with 2.3 million votes.

Sammy also had a good year in 2000, when his batting average was a solid .320. He hit 50 home runs and drove in 138 runs. And in 2001, he eclipsed the 60 home run mark again, making him the only player in major league history to hit more than 60 homers in three seasons. McGwire, plagued by injuries that slowed him in his final years in baseball, retired in 2001 with a total of 583 home runs over 16 seasons, a lifetime .263 batting average, and 1,414 RBI.

Gradually over the next four years, Sosa's batting average declined; he hit fewer home runs and drove in fewer runs, although still surpassing the 100 RBI mark in 2002 and 2003. In the disastrous 2004 season, however, his RBI total dropped to 80. He still hit 35 home runs, a respectable number, but his batting average dropped to .261. Sammy was hampered by other injuries, including a freak back sprain in May, caused by a couple of sneezes that put him out of the lineup for a month.

Sammy Sosa and Cubs manager Dusty Baker hug after Chicago defeated the Atlanta Braves, 5-1, in Game 5 of the 2003 National League Division series. By the 2004 season, Sosa had become disgruntled with Baker and Cubs management, and he was traded to the Baltimore Orioles in January 2005.

After that came a hip injury and a bicep sprain that affected both his fielding and hitting. He played in only 126 games, compared to 159 in 1998; his batting average of .261 was his lowest in 10 years; and his streak of nine straight years with more than 100 RBI came to an end when he only drove in 80 runs. He hit 35 home runs, which is a respectable number for average players, but Sammy Sosa had never been an average player. Then came the incident in which Sammy walked out of Wrigley Field in the first inning of the Cubs' final game with

Atlanta on October 3, 2004. He claimed he left the game in the seventh inning, but a video surveillance camera proved otherwise. For this behavior, he was fined $87,400—a day's pay.

Sammy told reporters he was tired of being blamed for the Cubs' never-ending problems. And the truth was, despite Sosa's outstanding performances with the Cubs over the years, the team never won a division championship and never came close to getting to the World Series. In 2004, the team came in third in the National League Central Division. Periodically, Sosa had complained that management seemed to think he could save the team all by himself. He wanted other power hitters in the lineup, and he wanted better pitching, a longstanding weakness for the Cubs.

His final manager in Chicago was Dusty Baker, who professed to be puzzled over Sosa's hostility toward him. Baker had been one of Sammy's strongest supporters and came to his defense after the corked-bat incident. He said at the time, "Deep down in my heart, I truly believe Sammy didn't know that was in there," he said. "But I just hope that this event, whatever it was, doesn't tarnish his career or take away all that Sammy Sosa's done—for baseball and for Chicago."[47] While Sosa complained when Baker dropped him to sixth in the batting lineup, aside from that specific complaint, his problems with Baker and the Cubs' management in general were difficult to pin down.

Trade rumors began during the 2004 season. Sammy himself wanted to be traded, and management began looking for likely teams. The New York Mets seemed like a possibility, because the general manager was Omar Minaya, a Dominican native who had signed Sosa to his first contract with the Texas Rangers in 1985. Then the Baltimore Orioles and manager Lee Mazzilli expressed interest in Sosa to bolster their offensive punch. Because Sosa was owed $25 million on a $72 million multiyear contract, the terms of the trade were expensive for the Cubs. The Cubs had to send the Orioles $16.15 million to carry out the deal. In the end, Sosa was traded for Jerry

Hairston Jr., a second baseman who had hit .303 in 2004 but didn't play every game, and two minor leaguers with potential. The Orioles wound up with two 500-plus home run hitters, Sosa (574) and Rafael Palmeiro (551), during the off-season. Both Sammy and the Chicago management seemed relieved by his departure, but the causes of his rift with the Cubs were never really explained. Dusty Baker met with his former star after the trade and came away just as puzzled as he was before. "We had a short conversation," Baker said. "I wished him well. I did ask him, 'Hey, man, I'm still bewildered about what happened and why.' He really didn't have an answer. He said, 'It's in the past. Good luck and God bless you.' That was the extent of the conversation."[48]

9

Good-bye Chicago, Hello Baltimore

On opening day of the 2005 season, the Baltimore fans were prepared to welcome Sammy Sosa. When he sprinted out to his position in right field, Sammy got a standing ovation from the 48,271 fans at the ballpark. In interviews after the trade, Sosa indicated that he was very happy to play in Baltimore, where Camden Yards, a state-of-the-art ballpark built in 1992, is as comfortable and batter-friendly as Wrigley Field, the second-oldest ballpark in the major leagues. Sammy seemed so determined to forget the past that in one interview he referred to the Chicago Cubs as "that other team I was on in Chicago."[49] In another interview, he said of Baltimore, "The best of Sammy Sosa is coming now. Whatever happened in Chicago, that was a good 13 years for me, but now I have a new house that I have to take care of."[50]

After Sammy was traded to the Baltimore Orioles before the 2005 season, Chicago fans were both pleased and saddened. An era was coming to a close. Everyone seemed to have a take on the story.

"Sammy Sosa gave us many great seasons and a lot of historic moments," Illinois governor Rod Blagojevich said on sports talk radio. "Because of that, he will one day be in the Hall of Fame. This is a sad way for the Sosa era to end in Chicago, but it's probably time for the Cubs and Sammy to go in different directions."[51] "He is going to be missed," said Cubs legend Ernie Banks. "I know things turned a little sour. It is just one of the unfortunate things that happen."[52] The *Chicago Tribune* reported that at Wrigleyville Sports, a souvenir shop at Addison Street and Sheffield Avenue, Sosa items sat on shelves untouched, despite the fact that they were marked down in price. A life-sized cardboard cutout of Sosa was stuck in a corner behind other merchandise, drawing no interest at $35.

In Baltimore, however, everything was sweetness and light. Sammy said he was happy to be with a new club, and the Orioles were happy with their new slugger. Orioles manager Lee Mazzilli said he was excited by Sosa's arrival. "It's a good time for us right now," he said, "and I think the city of Baltimore is going to see a young Sammy Sosa go out there and play. He has the stride, the determination, and a will to win. We're all hoping that Sammy's the guy that will take us over the top."[53] "Ah, he's exciting," said David Newhan, who played both the infield and outfield for the Orioles. "I liken him to a rock star, a movie-star type personality. He transcends everyone— the fans, even everyone playing alongside him. It's just fun to have that energy."[54]

But before he could start playing for his new team, the issue of steroid use raised its ugly head. And Sammy Sosa was unfortunately and perhaps unfairly touched by it.

THE STEROIDS ISSUE TAKES CENTER STAGE

The use of steroids to enhance performance has been an ongoing issue in baseball, as well as in other sports, but it really caught the eye of the public—not to mention the U.S. Congress—when Jose Canseco, the former Oakland A's player, wrote a book called *Juiced: Wild Times, Rampant 'Roids, Smash*

During the March 17, 2005, congressional hearing on steroids in Washington, D.C., several major league players denied using the banned substance to enhance their performance. Pictured here, left to right: Sammy Sosa, translator Patricia Rosell, former St. Louis Cardinal Mark McGwire, Baltimore Oriole first baseman Rafael Palmeiro, and Boston Red Sox pitcher Curt Schilling.

Hits and How Baseball Got Big. In it, Canseco recounted how steroid use among major league baseball players was widespread and related that he and Mark McGwire had used them when they played together at Oakland.

Along with many other players, Sammy Sosa vigorously denied that he used any performance-enhancing drugs. In fact,

he said if a testing policy were introduced in baseball he would
be first in line. Such a testing policy had in fact been introduced in 2002. It calls for periodic, unannounced testing of
players both during the season and in the off-season. Players
may be suspended if they test positive for steroids.

Congress held hearings in March 2005 and took testimony
from Mark McGwire and Sammy Sosa, among other players.
McGwire declined to admit or deny he used steroids, reading a
written statement and choking back tears. It was a stand that
was praised by Sosa. He said he respected McGwire's decision
not to respond to questions about steroid use. "Mark is a great
person, a person that I respect," [55] he said.

The issue of steroids in baseball actually had been simmer-
ing for a long time. In a famous confrontation in July 2002,
Sports Illustrated writer Rick Reilly challenged Sosa to take a
steroid test and gave him the address of a lab. Sosa was miffed.
Afterwards, Sosa commented, "I have worked hard all my life
to be what I am today. People now are pointing fingers to
everybody, because they think everybody that hits a home run
is on steroids."[56]

In April 2005, a group called Hispanics Across America
delivered a symbolic coffin to the New York office of baseball
commissioner Bud Selig to emphasize its demand that organized baseball do more to test Dominican prospects for drugs.
"If they send a message to the amateur players that before they
sign a contract they will be drug-tested, they will clean up the
system almost immediately,"[57] said Fernando Mateo, head of
the group. The demand acknowledged the fact that the
Dominican Republic sends more players to the major leagues
than any other Latino country.

And because of the controversy over steroids, a North
Dakota legislator in March 2005 introduced a resolution calling for the reinstatement of North Dakota's own Roger Maris
as the single-season home run record holder. Although the
move was mostly symbolic, it demonstrated how strongly
many people were beginning to feel about how much steroid

use had contributed to the amazing production of home runs in recent years and the bulking up of some players. McGwire, for instance, is 6-feet-5 and during his home run rampages weighed 250 pounds. He wasn't called "Big Mac" for nothing. By the time he testified before Congress in 2005, he had slimmed down considerably. Sosa, too, put on muscle during his career, but there has never been any evidence that he used performance-enhancing drugs. He insisted he bulked up by lifting weights and eating right. And after the major leagues cracked down on steroid use with periodic checking, he continued to hit home runs.

Guilt by Association

The first player suspended under Major League Baseball's new drug-testing policy was Cuban-born Alex Sanchez, of the Tampa Bay Devil Rays. Sanchez was suspended in April 2005 for 10 days after testing positive for steroids. He denied using steroids and pointed out that he is not a home run hitter. Sanchez, who arrived in the United States from Cuba on a raft, was valued for his speed and defensive skills. Under the policy, if a player tests positive a second time, he gets a 30-day suspension and 60 days if he tests positive a third time.

Anabolic steroids (anabolic means "building body tissue") were originally developed in the 1930s to help men whose bodies produced inadequate amounts of the natural hormone responsible for development of masculine characteristics. Some athletes found years ago that steroids could help them build muscle, increase endurance, and perform better. Bodybuilders were especially enthusiastic steroid users. Arnold Schwarzenegger, former bodybuilding champion and the current governor of California, has admitted using them.

Steroids have dangerous side effects, however; they can cause heart attacks, liver tumors, jaundice, fluid retention, high blood pressure, and homicidal rage (informally called 'roid rage). In fact, they can kill. Former NFL All-Pro football lineman Lyle Alzado blamed heavy steroid use for causing the brain cancer that killed him in 1992. Several bodybuilders died of conditions related to steroid use. Kenny "Flex" Wheeler, a four-time winner of the annual Arnold Classic bodybuilding contest, who admitted using steroids since the age of 18, said he believes they caused kidney problems that resulted in a kidney transplant. Other Arnold Classic competitors—Mohammed Benaziza, Paul Dillett, and Andreas Munzer—weren't so lucky. They died from conditions associated with steroid use.

Suspicions fell on Mark McGwire after his astounding home run production in the late 1990s. An Associated Press reporter found androstenedione in McGwire's locker. McGwire admitted using it as a dietary supplement. Androstenedione is a natural substance found in humans, animals, and even in the pollen of many plants. When taken orally, it is believed to increase blood levels of testosterone, the male sex hormone. Increased testosterone is effective in building muscle, increasing energy, and speeding up recovery time after strenuous exercise. It was legal when McGwire was using it, but it since has been banned by major league baseball.

Attention was also focused on the Giants' Barry Bonds, who broke McGwire's record with 73 homers in 2002. Throughout much of the 2005 season, he was laid up after knee surgery, but entering the 2006 season, he needs only 6 homers to reach Babe Ruth's career total of 714 and 47 to reach Hank Aaron's 755. "I think people would be devastated to think that 1998 is not what we thought it was, that it was in some way a fabrication of the truth," said Peter Roby, director of the Center for the Study of Sport in Society at Northeastern University in Boston. "When people come to love someone and then find that they have been in another relationship, their trust has been violated."[58]

Unfortunately, for players like Mark McGwire and Sammy Sosa, the mere fact that they were called to testify before a congressional committee investigating drug use in organized baseball made people wonder. Lawyers call it "guilt by association."

Sammy Sosa is all smiles during his press conference in Baltimore on February 2, 2005, shortly after he was traded from the Chicago Cubs to the Orioles. Unfortunately, Sosa battled a toe injury throughout the 2005 season and hit just .221, with 14 home runs and 45 RBI.

A NEW SEASON

Sammy's new city, Baltimore, has been the home of some of the country's most fanatical baseball fans, dating back to the nineteenth century, but over the decades the fans frequently were frustrated by the city's inability to hold on to a major league team. The city has been home to several professional baseball teams, in both the major and minor leagues. The most recent and longest lasting Baltimore Orioles team debuted in 1954, after the city had gone more than 50 years without a team. And in 2005, Sammy Sosa was bouncing home run balls off the parked jets at the executive airfield next to the Orioles' training camp in Fort Lauderdale, Florida, as the team prepared for a new season.

Sammy's locker in Baltimore was next to that of fellow Dominican Miguel Tejada, the hard-hitting shortstop who was the American League's Most Valuable Player in 2002, when he played for the Oakland A's. He led the majors in RBI with 150 in 2004. Sosa was confident he was gong to have a big rebound year. "Oh yeah, I'm having a good time," he told reporters in Florida. "Everything is looking pretty good. I feel great. I like to be around the guys. Everyone is together. I feel great about it, the way it worked out for me here. All these guys are great."[59]

Sammy went homerless in the Orioles' first six games, his customary slow start. But he was hitting the ball. His batting average climbed to .299 after just 19 games. And his two home runs in a game against the Toronto Blue Jays on April 24, 2005, gave him 67 multihomer games in his career, tying him with Mark McGwire and putting him just behind Barry Bonds's 68 and Babe Ruth's 72. "On one side, it's very nice to be in that category," Sosa told reporters, "but right now, for myself, I have no time to celebrate. It's just the beginning of the year. There's still a long way to go."[60]

Sammy met with some Chicago sports reporters in Baltimore on May 1. It was the first time he had seen the press from his former city since he was traded. They were in the Baltimore area to cover the Chicago Bulls-Washington Wizards National Basketball Association playoff series. They tracked down Sosa and asked him, basically, how it was going. "I know my legacy is there," he said when asked about his time in Chicago. "But I'm here now and I'm having fun. One of the things that's happening here I'm so proud of is every day it's a new hero," he said. "That's the whole team together. We've got great people around here."[61]

Unfortunately, the team chemistry that seemed so promising in May quickly faded after injuries and off-the-field problems began to take their toll. Despite starting the season strong—the Orioles led the American League East after the first 62 days—the team finished 74-88, good for fourth place in the American League East. The Orioles were banking on the veteran combination of Sosa and Rafael Palmeiro—the first teammates in the history of the game with more than 500 home runs apiece—to help carry the team, but Palmeiro tested positive for steroids in early August and was forced to serve a 10-game suspension. Sosa, meanwhile, battled a toe injury all season and spent two stints on the disabled list; the second of which caused him to miss the last month and a half of the season. In addition to Sosa's injury problems, starting catcher Javy Lopez was hindered by a broken hand and starting pitcher Sidney Ponson struggled with off-the-field issues.

In August 2005, the Orioles replaced manager Lee Mazzilli with Sam Perlozzo, just three days after Palmeiro was suspended for using steroids. Perlozzo won his first game as manager, with the Orioles beating Los Angeles partly on the strength of a home run by Sammy. Although Sosa struggled through his least productive season as an everyday major league player, Perlozzo believes Sammy's work ethic will help him get back on track in 2006. "Sammy Sosa never says that he wants a day off. He plays hard every day and does everything you ask,"[62] said Perlozzo.

Unquestionably, Sammy's 2005 season with the Orioles was a disappointment to him, his team, and the fans, who expected great things from the slugger when the season began. He batted an anemic .221, with a mere 14 home runs and 45 RBI. The onetime speed demon on the bases stole only one base. He sat out the last several weeks of the season with a toe injury.

There were rumors he might go to Japan to play, but he rejected that notion after the season ended. He also appeared not to be contemplating retirement. He said in an interview in the *Washington Post* on October 5 that he planned to remain in major league baseball so he could reach the 600 home run mark. He needed only 12 more to attain that feat; one that only Babe Ruth, Hank Aaron, Barry Bonds, and Willie Mays had surpassed.

Whether he would remain with the Orioles was a doubtful prospect. But he said he would like to stay in the American League where he could be a designated hitter. There is no such position in the National League. Serving as a DH would enable him to get some at-bats in his quest to reach the 600 mark. Additionally, a designated hitter does not have to play in the field, which limits the opportunity for injury and could potentially give Sammy a few more years in the major leagues.

Regardless of where Sammy ends up, he is determined to put the 2005 season behind him: "Next year I know I will be better," he stated after the conclusion of the season.

Chronology and Timeline

1968   Samuel Peralta Sosa born November 12, in Consuelo, Dominican Republic; he is the fifth of seven children of Juan Montero and Lucretia (Mireya) Sosa.

1975   Father dies on August 30.

1978   Family moves to Santo Domingo.

1981   Family moves to San Pedro de Macoris; Sammy given first baseball glove by factory owner Bill Chase.

1982   Hits first two home runs in Nelson Rodriguez amateur league in San Pedro.

1984   Signed by Phillies scout but nothing comes of it; has tryouts with New York Yankees, New York Mets, Montreal Expos, and Toronto Blue Jays.

1985   Signed by Texas Rangers as amateur free agent.

1989   On June 16, called up from the minor leagues for first time and appears in first major league game in Yankee Stadium versus New York Yankees; on June 21, hits first home run against Roger Clemens in Fenway Park, Boston; on July 29, traded by Rangers with Wilson Alvarez and Scott Fletcher to Chicago White Sox for Harold Baines and Fred Manriquel; on August 22, hits second career home run as a White Sox.

1991   Marries Sonia Rodriguez.

1992   Traded to Chicago Cubs with Ken Patterson for Dominican legend George Bell.

1993   Has perfect game, six hits in six at-bats against Rockies on Fourth of July weekend; named National League Player of Week for first time; in September, reaches "30/30" mark, more than 30 home runs and 30 stolen bases; signs one-year contract for $2.95 million.

1994   On August 11, baseball strike starts, season cancelled.

1995 On July 2, named to All-Star team for first time; attains "30/30" second time.

1996 In January, signs three-year contract for $16 million; in July, named National League Player of the Month; on August 20, season ends with broken bone in hand.

1997 Signed to four-year, $42.5-million contract; starts working on his swing with hitting coach Jeff Pentland.

1998 In June, hits 20 home runs, breaking 61-year record for most home runs in a month; on September 13, hits sixty-first and sixty-second home runs to break Roger Maris's record of 61; finishes season with 66 home runs to Mark McGwire's 70; named National League Most Valuable Player; his Sammy Sosa Charitable Foundation sends aid to Dominican Republic hit by Hurricane Georges; given Roberto Clemente Man of the Year award for charitable activities.

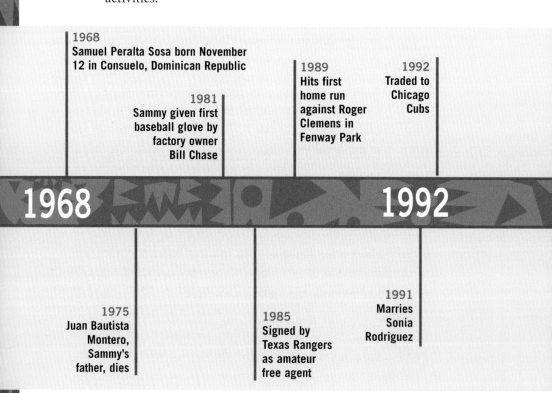

1968
Samuel Peralta Sosa born November 12 in Consuelo, Dominican Republic

1981
Sammy given first baseball glove by factory owner Bill Chase

1989
Hits first home run against Roger Clemens in Fenway Park

1992
Traded to Chicago Cubs

1968

1992

1975
Juan Bautista Montero, Sammy's father, dies

1985
Signed by Texas Rangers as amateur free agent

1991
Marries Sonia Rodriguez

1999 Becomes first player to hit more than 60 home runs in two seasons.

2000 Restructures his Charitable Foundation after *Fortune* magazine article says it is a financial mess.

2001 Hits 64 home runs to become only major league player to hit more than 60 in three seasons and first to hit at least 50 in four consecutive seasons.

2003 On April 4, hits five hundredth home run in Cincinnati, first Latino player to do so; on June 3, ejected from game against Tampa Bay Devil Rays for using corked bat; ends season with record nine consecutive seasons with more than 100 RBI.

2004 On October 3, leaves final game of season early, fined one-day's pay, $87,500; batting average drops to .253, with 35 home runs and 80 RBI.

1995
Named to first All-Star team

1998
Breaks Roger Maris's single-season record of 61 home runs and finishes season with 66 home runs

2003
Becomes first Latino player to hit 500 career home runs

1995

2005

2005
Traded to Baltimore Orioles, but hits just .221, with 14 home runs and 45 RBI

1997
Signs four-year, $42.5-million contract with Cubs

2001
Hits 64 home runs to become only major league player to hit more than 60 in three seasons

2005 On January 28, traded to Baltimore Orioles for Jerry Hairston Jr. and two rookies; plays in only 102 games for the Orioles because of a toe injury and hits just .221, with 14 home runs and 45 RBI.

Notes

Chapter 1

1 Bill Gutman, *Sammy Sosa: A Biography* (New York: Pocket Books, 1998), 36.
2 Ibid., 59.
3 Sammy Sosa, *Sosa: An Autobiography* (New York: Warner Books, 2000), 1.
4 *Philadelphia Inquirer*, June 6, 2003.

Chapter 2

5 Gutman, *Sammy Sosa*, xi.

Chapter 3

6 Sosa, *An Autobiography*, 49.
7 Ibid., 45.
8 Ibid., 56.
9 Ibid., 105.

Chapter 4

10 Sosa, *An Autobiography*, 143.
11 Ibid., 142. Pete Rose, retired player-manager of the Cincinnati Reds and former Phillies infielder, holds the major league record of 4,256 lifetime base hits. He was banned from baseball for life in 1989 for betting on games.
12 Ibid., 145.
13 *Cincinnati Enquirer*, August 12, 2004.
14 Sosa, *An Autobiography*, 152.
15 Ibid., 159.

Chapter 5

16 Ibid., 162.
17 Ibid., 169.
18 *Baseball Digest*, June 2002.
19 Ibid.
20 Sosa, *An Autobiography*, 169.
21 Ibid., 170.
22 Ibid., 172.
23 Ibid., 173.
24 Ibid., 174.

25 Ibid., 177.
26 Ibid.
27 Ibid., 178.
28 Ibid., 181.
29 Ibid., 183.

Chapter 6

30 Gutman, Sammy Sosa, 84.
31 Ibid., 88.
32 Ibid., 89.

Chapter 7

33 Gutman, *Sammy Sosa*, 92.
34 Ibid., 94.
35 Ibid., 127.
36 Sosa, *An Autobiography*, 193.
37 Gutman, *Sammy Sosa*, 134.
38 Ibid., 135.
39 Sosa, *An Autobiography*, 195.
40 Gutman, *Sammy Sosa*, 140, 141.
41 *Latino Legends in Sports* (*http://www.latinosportslegends. com*), August 5, 2000.

Chapter 8

42 Sosa, *An Autobiography*, 202, 203.
43 Gutman, *Sammy Sosa*, 140, 141.
44 Ibid., 142.
45 *Latino Legends in Sports*, August 5, 2000.
46 Sosa, 202, 203.
47 *Chicago Tribune*, January 30, 2005.
48 *Chicago Tribune*, February 18, 2005.

Chapter 9

49 *Centre Daily Times* (State College, Pa.), March 2, 2005.
50 WBAL Channel. February 2, 2005.
51 *Chicago Tribune*, January 30, 2005.
52 Ibid.
53 Ibid.

54 *Centre Daily Times* (State College, Pa.), March 2, 2005.
55 *Centre Daily Times* (State College, Pa.), March 2, 2005.
56 *Baltimore Sun*, April 25, 2005.
57 Associated Press, April 15, 2005.
58 *New York Times*, March 15, 2005.
59 *Baltimore Sun*, April 25, 2005.
60 Ibid.
61 Associated Press, May 1, 2005.
62 Jeff Zribiec, "Perlozzo Ponders Way to Warm Up Chilly Bat of Sosa," *Baltimore Sun*, August 16, 2005.

Bibliography

Books

Chernow, Barbara A., and George A. Vallasi, eds. *The Columbia Encyclopedia*. New York: Columbia University Press, 1993.

Driscoll, Laura. *Sammy Sosa: He's The Man*. New York: Grosset & Dunlap, 1999.

Gutman, Bill. *Sammy Sosa: A Biography*. New York: Simon & Schuster, 1998.

Harvey, Shawn. *The Rough Guide to the Dominican Republic*. New York: The Penguin Group, 2002.

Piparo, C.A. *Mark McGwire: Home Run King*. Ridgewood, N.J.: Infinity Plus One, 1999.

Sosa, Sammy. *Sosa: An Autobiography*. New York: Warner Books, 2000.

Newspapers, Magazines, and Wire Services

Associated Press

Baltimore Sun

Centre Daily Times (State College, Pa.)

Chicago Tribune

Cincinnati Enquirer

Fortune

Latino Legends in Sports

National Magazine of the Successful Latino

New York Daily News

New York Times

Philadelphia Daily News

Philadelphia Inquirer

San Francisco Examiner

Sporting News

Sports Illustrated

Further Reading

Albritton, Christine. *Sammy's Season*. Chicago, Ill.: Contemporary Books Inc., 1999.

Gutman, Bill. *Sammy Sosa: A Biography*. New York: Simon & Schuster, 1998.

Honor, Books. *Slammin Sammy Sosa!: The Race for the Record*. Trade Life Books, 1998.

Sosa, Sammy. *Sosa: An Autobiography*. New York: Warner Books, 2000.

Sports Illustrated. *Home Run Heroes: Mark McGwire, Sammy Sosa, and a Season for the Ages*. New York: Simon & Schuster, 1998.

Staff of the Chicago Tribune. *Out of the Blue: The Remarkable Story of the 2003 Chicago Cubs*. Chicago, Ill.: Triumph Books, 2003.

Web sites

Baseball Information
  http://baseball-reference.com/

The Eclectic Baseball Magazine
  http://thediamondangle.com/

ESPN Sports Network
  http://www.espn.go.com/

Hickocksports.com
  http://www.hickocksports.com

Infoplease.com
  http://www.Infoplease.com/

Major League Baseball's Official Site
  http://mlb.mlb.com/NASApp/mlb/index.jsp

National Baseball Hall of Fame and Museum
  http://baseballhalloffame.org/

NBC 11, Baltimore
  http://www.thewbalchannel.com/index.html

The Official Baseball History Site
  http://baseball-almanac.com/

The Stories behind the Stats
  http://www.baseballlibrary.com/baseballlibrary/

Index

1919 "Black Sox" scandal, 8

Aaron, Hank, 63, 96, 99
Acevedo, Francisco, 29
Alexander, Manny, 57
Alzado, Lyle, 95
Andujar, Joaquin, 23
Aparicio, Luis, 19
Arizona Diamondbacks, 69
Atlanta Braves, 28–29, 47, 72, 82, 88–89

Baines, Harold, 35–36
Baker, Dusty, 88–90
Balderson, Dick, 19
Baltimore, Orioles, 11
  and Sosa, 88–92, 97–99
Banks, Ernie, 41, 92
Baseball, Major League
  American league, 6, 19, 31, 33, 36, 60, 62, 64, 98–99
  fans, 7, 9, 44, 97
  game of strategy, 8–9
  history, 6, 11, 15, 18–19, 63, 80
  National league, 6, 10, 18–19, 33, 38, 40–41, 43, 46–48, 50–53, 55, 63–64, 66–67, 72, 77, 81–82, 88–89, 100
  strike of 1994, 6–8, 44–46, 72, 75
  World series, 7–9, 41–42, 46, 62–63, 89
Beck, Rod, 57, 82
Bell, George, 23–24, 39–40, 43
Bell, James Thomas "Cool Papa," 25–27
Bellan, Esteban, 18
Benaziza, Mohammed, 96
Bench, Johnny, 16
Blagojevich, Rod, 92

Blauser, Jeff, 67
Boehringer, Brian, 77
Bonds, Barry, 11, 52–53, 96, 98–99
Boston Red Sox, 8, 33, 62–64, 93
  Fenway Park, 34
Breton, Marcos, 19, 77
Brown, Kevin, 87
Brown, Mordecai "Three Finger," 41
Browning, Roger, 86
Buechele, Steve, 42–43
Bush, George W., 13

California Angels, 36
Canseco, Jose
  Juiced: Wild Times, Rampant 'Roids, Smash Hits and How Baseball Got Big, 92–93
Caray, Harry, 45
Carlton, Steve, 66
Carty, Rico, 24, 28
Castillo, Felipe, 32
Castro, Luis, 18
Cepeda, Orlando, 19, 26
Cepeda, Perucho, 26
Chance, Frank, 41
Chase, William, 21–23, 30, 86
Chicago Cubs, 32, 63
  curse, 40–42
  and Sosa, 9–10, 13–14, 33, 38–40, 42–50, 52–53, 56–58, 65–67, 69–82, 86–91, 97–98
  Wrigley Field, 13–14, 40–42, 46, 48, 51–52, 67, 69, 74, 79–81, 86, 88, 91
Chicago White Sox, 8, 43
  and Sosa, 35–38
Cincinnati Reds, 16, 18, 72, 80–81

Ciudad Trujillo Dragones, 25–28
Clark, Mark, 65
Clemens, Roger, 34, 65
Clemente, Roberto, 13, 19, 83
Clinton, Bill, 12–13, 82
Cobb, Ty, 63
Colorado Rockies, 19, 42, 47
Columbus, Christopher, 24–25
Concepción, Dave, 16
Consuelo, Dominican Republic
  Sosa's boyhood in, 17, 21
Cruz, Mickey, 32

Dawson, Andre, 40
Detroit Tigers, 12, 36, 41, 63, 67, 69
Dihigo, Martin, 19
Dillett, Paul, 96
Dinzey, Amado, 30
Domingo (baseball team), 26, 28
Dominican Republic, 16, 87
  and baseball, 11–12, 17, 18–20, 23–29, 33–34, 39, 48, 54, 70, 76, 80–81, 89, 94
  history, 24–28, 84–85
  relief efforts in, 13, 81–83, 86
Durocher, Leo, 41

Evers, Johnny, 41

Fernandez, Tony, 24
Florida Marlins, 52–53, 66–67, 72
Foster, George, 16
Foxx, Jimmie, 64
Franco, Julio, 23–24, 33

Gaetti, Gary, 81
Gant, Ron, 46
Gehrig, Lou, 62–64
Gibson, Josh, 25–27
Giuliani, Rudolph, 12
Glavine, Tom, 44
Gonzalez, Juan, 31–32
Gonzalez, Luis, 47
Gonzalez, Ozzie, 33
Grace, Mark, 46, 76
Greenburg, Hank, 64
Greenlee, Gus, 27
Griffey, Ken, Jr., 52
   and the home run
      record, 6, 9, 11, 16,
      57, 59, 64–66, 70–71,
      77
Guerrero, Pedro, 24

Hagler, Marvin, 22
Hairston, Jerry, Jr., 90
Hawkins, Andy, 34
Hearns, Thomas, 22
Himes, Larry, 36, 38–40,
   43–44, 46
Hispaniola, 24–25
Houston Astros, 65, 71,
   76, 81
Hriniak, Walt, 38
Hutton, Mark, 52

Incaviglia, Pete, 34

John Paul II, Pope, 13
Johnson, Lance, 57, 81
Johnson, Randy, 71, 87
Jordan, Michael, 79, 81

LaSorda, Tommy, 48–49
Latin America
   and baseball, 18–19, 27,
      32–33, 54, 72, 74, 94
Lefebvre, Jim, 42
Leonard, Sugar Ray, 22
Licey (baseball team), 25
Lima, Jose, 81

Los Angeles Dodgers, 46,
   49, 99
Luque, Adolfo, 18

Maddux, Greg, 40
Manoguayabo,
   Dominican Republic,
   33
Mantle, Mickey, 8, 60–61
Marichal, Juan, 18–19
Maris, Roger, 60
   home run record, 6–8,
      11, 57, 59, 61–62, 64,
      69, 71, 73–76, 94
Martinez, Dennis, 40
Martinez, Pedro, 33
Mateo, Fernando, 94
May, Derrick, 42
Mays, Willie, 45–46, 99
Mazzilli, Lee, 89, 92, 99
McGwire, Mark, 37
   and the home run
      record, 6–7, 9, 11, 16,
      44, 57, 59–61, 64–67,
      69–83, 86–87, 98
   steroid scandal, 14, 79,
      93–96
Mieske, Matt, 81
Milwaukee Brewers, 7,
   67, 74, 76, 80
Minaya, Omar, 30, 32, 89
Minnesota Twins, 36, 66
Moehler, Brian, 69
Montero, Juan Bautista
   (father), 17
   death, 20
Montreal Expos, 29, 40,
   57, 81
Morandini, Mickey, 42,
   57
Morgan, Joe, 16, 81
Morgan, Mike, 73
Munzer, Andreas, 96

National Baseball Hall of
   Fame, 14, 19, 27, 41,
   63, 92

Negro Leagues, 19, 27
Newhan, David, 92
New York Mets, 29–30,
   53, 76, 81, 89
New York Yankees, 8, 29,
   32, 34, 60–64

Oakland Athletics, 6, 37,
   57, 59, 92–93, 98
Obuchi, Keizo, 13
Oliva, Tony, 19
Overall, Orval, 41
Ozersky, Philip, 75

Paige, Satchel, 25–28
Palmeiro, Rafael, 90, 93,
   98–99
Peguero, Hector, 28–29
Pentland, Jeff, 10, 53–58,
   65, 76, 87
Perez, Tony, 16
Perlozzo, Sam, 99
Philadelphia Phillies, 29,
   66–67
Pittsburgh Pirates, 40,
   51, 53, 72, 83
Plunk, Eric, 76
Ponson, Sidney, 99
Power, Vic, 19

Rawley, Shane, 36
Reilly, Rick, 94
Riggleman, Jim, 45–46,
   51–52
Robinson, Jackie, 18–19
Rodriguez, Henry, 57
Rodriquez, Torivio, 81
Rose, Pete, 16, 43
Ruth, George Herman
   "Babe," 13, 75, 99
   fans, 8
   home run record, 8, 59,
      61–64, 72, 74, 96, 98
Sammy Sosa Charitable
   Foundation, 12, 81,
   83

medical foundation, 83, 86
Samuel, Juan, 24
Sanchez, Alex, 95
Sanchez, Rey, 32, 46
Sandberg, Ryne, 47
San Diego Padres, 45–46, 77–78
San Pedro de Macoris, Dominican Republic, 57
   baseball team, 25, 28
   residents honor Sosa, 13
   Sosa's hometown, 11–12, 16–17, 21, 23–24, 30, 33, 48, 72, 79, 81, 84, 86
Santo Domingo, Dominican Republic, 20–21, 25, 30, 48, 84
Santos, Valerio De Los, 74
Schilling, Curt, 87, 93
Schmidt, Jason, 72
Schwarzenegger, Arnold, 95
Seattle Mariners, 57, 64, 71
Seaver, Tom, 66
Selig, Bud, 46, 79, 94
Sierra, Ruben, 33
Sisler, George, 64
Sosa, Kenia (daughter), 38
Sosa, Keysha (daughter), 38

Sosa, Lucretia (mother), 17, 20–21, 30, 48, 79, 84
   influence of, 22
Sosa, Luis (brother), 17
   influence of, 20, 28
Sosa, Michael (son), 38
Sosa, Samuel Peralta
   awards and honors, 11–13, 50–53, 66–68, 79–80, 82–83, 87
   birth, 17
   boyhood, 12, 16–22
   chronology and time-line, 101–104
   corked-bat scandal, 14, 89
   critics, 54–55, 67
   fans, 11, 13–15, 42, 45, 66, 87, 91–92
   early career, 9–11, 23–58, 65
   and the home run record, 7, 9–10, 16, 44, 59–61, 69–79, 81–83, 86–87
   philanthropy, 12, 80–86
   quirks, 13–14
   statistics, 10–12, 31, 34–38, 40, 42–48, 50–52, 54–55, 58, 68, 78, 82, 87–88, 97–99
   steroid scandal, 14, 79, 92–96
Sosa, Sammy Jr. (son), 38
Sosa, Sonia Rodriguez (wife), 38–39, 79

Stallard, Tracy, 62
Sterner, Daniel, 86
St. Louis Cardinals, 6–7, 46, 57, 62, 64–65, 73–75, 81, 93

Tampa Bay Devil Rays, 32, 95
Tapani, Kevin, 57, 65
Tejada, Miguel, 97
Texas Rangers
   and Sosa, 13, 19, 30–35, 89
Tinker, Joe, 41
Toronto Blue Jays, 29, 39, 98
Trachsel, Steve, 57, 65, 74
Trujillo, Rafael Leonidas Molina, 25–27
Trujillo, Ramfis, 25
Vanover, Larry, 42
Versalles, Zoilo, 19
Virgil, Ozzie, 18

Weeghman, Charles, 41
Wells, David, 66
Wheeler, Kenny "Flex," 96
Wilkinson, Bud, 60
Williams, Billy, 10, 48, 70
Wilson, Hack, 41, 72
Wood, Kerry, 57, 65–66
Wrigley, William, 41

York, Rudy, 12, 67, 69

About the Author

John Morrison is a longtime Philadelphia newspaperman. He has worked as a reporter, rewriteman, and editor. He has published poetry, short stories, and has written several books for Chelsea House, including *Syria*, in the series CREATION OF THE MODERN MIDDLE EAST, and *Frida Kahlo*, in the series THE GREAT HISPANIC HERITAGE.

Picture Credits